GETTING
EVEN

The Truth About
Workplace Revenge
— And How to Stop It

Thomas M. Tripp & Robert J. Bies

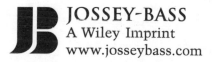

JOSSEY-BASS
A Wiley Imprint
www.josseybass.com

Published by Jossey-Bass.
A Wiley Imprint
989 Market Street, San Francisco, CA 94103-1741—www.josseybass.com

Jossey-Bass books and products are available through most bookstores. To contact Jossey-Bass directly call our Customer Care Department within the U.S. at 800-956-7739, outside the U.S. at 317-572-3986, or fax 317-572-4002.

Jossey-Bass also publishes its books in a variety of electronic formats. Some content that appears in print may not be available in electronic books.

Library of Congress Cataloging-in-Publication Data

Tripp, Thomas M., 1962-
  Getting even : the truth about workplace revenge and how to stop it / Thomas M. Tripp, Robert J. Bies.
    p. cm.
  Includes bibliographical references and index.
  ISBN 978-0-470-33967-1 (cloth)
  1. Organizational behavior. 2. Anger in the workplace. 3. Revenge. 4. Interpersonal confrontation. I. Bies, Rob
Title.
  HD58.7.T742 2009
  658.3'82dc22

                                2008041896

Printed in the United States of America
FIRST EDITION

HB Printing   10 9 8 7 6 5 4 3 2 1

Contents

To Jodi, Chloe, and Charlie, and to Susan, Kelly, and Brian

Preface

When we began our research on revenge almost fifteen years ago, our colleagues thought we were crazy. We would be pariahs among academics to study such a taboo or verboten subject, we were told, particularly by colleagues who were well-ensconced in business schools. Despite such warnings and concerns, we marched on. We marched to the tune of real people working in organizations who shared stories with us about the human and social reality of revenge in the workplace. We listened to their experiences and realized we had entered territory that was central to the well-being of companies today—yet left virtually unexplored in academic business literature.

From the very first study, the results of which we presented at the Stanford Trust Conference in 1994 (hosted by our colleague and friend, Rod Kramer), we knew we had touched on a topic that was very real and very human. We were greatly encouraged by the reaction of Gene Webb, the Stanford Business School professor who'd been an inspiring influence on Bob in his doctoral program. After hearing Bob present our results, Gene said, "You are on to something here. I will be the first to cite your work in one of my papers." That was the ultimate compliment and validation from a great man and scholar.

Since the early 1990s, we have conducted more than a dozen studies together and published the results. We have broadened the research to include other colleagues who shared our interest in revenge and related topics, such as forgiveness. From these studies, we began to see a clear pattern emerging about how people deal with frustration and injustice in everyday work life. That pattern undergirds our theoretical framework on how and why revenge occurs, which we describe in this book. While the facts, research findings, and stories we share are entertaining and persuasive, it is the theory that is most memorable and useful. After all, as Charles O. Whitman once put it, "Theory without facts is fantasy, but facts without theory is chaos!"

To bring our theory to life in this book, we drew from a database of almost eight hundred stories from the nearly five hundred employees and managers we've interviewed over the years. While all the stories are true, all names in the stories are fictitious. We changed all names to protect our interviewees' identities—and their guilt or innocence. But it is these people we want to particularly thank because they enlightened us about what is really going on in the trenches of working America.

In writing this book, as was the case in conducting our research, we have been a true partnership and collaboration. In this book, each of us was contributing equally and uniquely. More important, we have deepened and enriched our friendship in ways that we could not have imagined before we began this journey.

But, as Althea Gibson reminds us, "No matter what accomplishments you make, somebody helps you." And we have many people to acknowledge for their help with this book We thank Karl Aquino and Rod Kramer, who collaborated with us on our revenge research, making us much smarter as a result. We thank Max Bazerman and Roy Lewicki for their very helpful advice on writing books for a broader audience outside academia. In particular, we are grateful to Roy Lewicki for connecting us with the people at Jossey-Bass, our publisher.

Jossey-Bass editors Rebecca Browning and Byron Schneider provided thoughtful and incisive guidance, and we are grateful for their support and encouragement of us and our ideas. We especially thank Lucy McCauley for her detailed editing help on earlier drafts. Lucy helped us make our writing and our ideas come alive. Finally, the copyeditor polished and enhanced our writing, taking it to an even higher level of clarity and precision. Indeed, in every aspect of writing and producing this book, Jossey-Bass has been first-class in its working relationship with us.

Finally, our friends and family provided valuable feedback on earlier drafts, and we are especially indebted to Steve Besser, Susan Bies, Amy Skinner, and Jim Tripp. More important, though, our families supported us, putting up with time away from them so that we could meet the deadlines necessary to get this book done. Our heartfelt gratitude and love to Jodi, Chloe, and Charlie—and to Susan, Kelly, and Brian.

Thomas Tripp and Robert Bies, Fall 2008

Getting Even

1

AN INTRODUCTION TO REVENGE IN THE WORKPLACE

I give decaf to people who are rude to me.
—*Coffee barista, Portland, Oregon*

Beware how you treat your server if you value your morning coffee—or how your mechanic repairs your car, or a technician fixes your computer. As the confession from the disgruntled worker reveals in the quote that opens this chapter, such revenge is more common than you might care to believe. It often is the little nasty things, sometimes harmless, sometimes not, that employees do to a customer when they feel offended or mistreated. And often the customers never know what happened to them (adding to the joy of the avenging employee).

Acts of workplace revenge are not limited to customer-service encounters, of course. Indeed, they are commonplace, part of the social fabric of the workplace. What's more, such revenge is often triggered by seemingly mundane events—the small insults, the public put-downs, confrontations, and reprimands that most people experience on the job at some point. But larger issues come into play as well. Consider the following:

- A boss takes credit for the ideas of a subordinate, who responds by bad-mouthing the boss to others in the company.

- A successful middle manager at a consumer products company is fired summarily and without being

1

given a clear reason. Shocked by the action and
the treatment, the manager sues the company for
wrongful termination and discrimination.

- In an effort to help the boss, an employee mentions that
morale among workers is low. Like many who receive such
bad news, rather than reacting with gratitude, the boss
severely chastises the employee. After that, the employee
decides not to warn the boss about another impending
complaint—and then relishes senior management's public
chastisement of the boss when they hear the complaint.

- Upon vacating the White House in January 2001, Clinton
administration staffers, upset that that Republicans had
beat the Democrats in the elections, removed or damaged
the "W" keys on computer keyboards throughout the
White House—so when George W. Bush took office,
the new staffers could not type his nickname, "W."[1]

- An administrator for a fast-food franchise company
publicly berates a market manager for failing to meet
efficiency, sales, and profit targets. The manager, humiliated and embarrassed, vows to work harder and longer
hours to "get even" by proving the boss wrong.

These five true examples came from workplaces in different kinds of settings, and they each yielded different kinds of
outcomes. Yet they share two key traits. All resulted from the
same motivating desire: to get even. And none of these acts of
workplace revenge were violent—however destructive they still
may have been.

Does this surprise you? It surprises many of our students and
our audiences at conferences and corporate training presenta-
tions. In fact, these points are where our view of workplace
revenge, based on fifteen years of investigation, differs from much
of the current research. And they usually raise some immediate
questions.

First, if we contend that revenge is the common motivating desire in all these examples, how would our last story of the fast-food company manager qualify? Surely when there's such a positive outcome—an employee working harder!—we can't call that "workplace revenge," right? More to the point, why should an organization worry about revenge that benefits it, or at least appears to do so? Similarly, the Clinton White House example could be considered simply a case of lighthearted pranksterism. Or could it?

Revenge as we define it is *an action in response to some perceived harm or wrongdoing by another party, which is intended to inflict damage, injury, discomfort, or punishment on the party judged responsible.*[2] We suggest that all five opening examples meet this definition. They also all harbor at their core a strong *emotional* response—which, when it comes to workplace situations, spells trouble. Why? For one thing, when emotions are a primary driving factor, positive intentions can easily escalate into bad behavior. For another, even what starts as a harmless prank can be risky; things can all too easily go awry, and the result might not be harmless regardless of the intent. (Just ask the computer techs who spent countless hours and massive amounts of resources fixing or replacing keyboards in the White House!)

In any case, whether you perceive the outcome of a particular instance of revenge as positive, negative, or harmless, we believe it is wise to pay attention to all forms of revenge in the workplace. Why? Because at best revenge signals that something's a bit off-kilter in the organization—and at worst, that things have gone deeply wrong, systemwide. Later in this chapter and throughout the book, we explore in more detail how revenge affects the organization and what managers and leaders can do about that.

But what of our second point? If we're talking here about workplace revenge, why aren't we examining primarily *violent* kinds of revenge? After all, most people think of revenge as volatile behavior, an irrational response in a civilized organization or society.[3] But contrary to what many people may believe, violent forms of workplace revenge are extremely rare.[4] The sensational headlines and TV news stories we've all seen, disturbing as they are, are not the norm.* What we want to explore in this book are the everyday, all-too-common, and insidious forms of workplace revenge that can cause untold damage—and are worth managers' and organizations' close attention.

Let us be clear, then: this is not a book about workplace violence. Workplace revenge does not equal violence, except in very unusual and extreme cases. Most workplace revenge is not violent,[5] and most workplace violence is not motivated by revenge. If it were, we would expect most workplace homicides to be committed by employees and coworkers. But they're not. A 2000 Bureau of Labor Statistics report of workplace homicides from 1995 to 1999, for instance, showed that 44 percent of workplace homicides were armed robbery, where the assailant and victim did not even know each other; only 8 percent of homicides were committed by coworkers or former coworkers.[6] In 1993, of the 1,063 workplace homicides, only 59 involved coworkers.[7] So, when thinking of workplace violence, don't imagine a disgruntled postal worker (see box); imagine an armed robbery of a cash-laden taxi driver (which, according to the same report, is the most dangerous occupation in the United States, carrying the highest risk of being murdered on the job).

Going Postal

The image of U.S. postal workers gunning down former coworkers and bosses has become the public's favorite example of revenge gone awry in today's society.[8] That's why it's called "going postal." But does the U.S. Postal Service really have a corner on this particular form of revenge,

---

*For instance, according to the Bureau of Labor Statistics, in 2006 (the last year for which data are available at the time of writing), there were only 754 workplace assaults and violent acts in the entire United States. And 2006 was not an atypical year.

or have the media just made it appear so? Consider the statistics. In the past twenty-five years there have been nineteen incidents where a U.S. postal worker or former postal worker shot postal employees. And while that's nineteen incidents too many, statistically speaking it's less than one incident per year in an organization that employs 700,000–800,000 people. Clearly, it's a very rare problem.

By the way, it may surprise you to know that on a per capita basis, the U.S. Postal Service has no more than an *average* rate of "going postal" in the United States. Maybe less. In its own defense, the Postal Service reported that postal workers are only one-third as likely to be murdered at work as the average employee (that is, 0.26 versus 0.77 per 100,000 workers—though this statistic includes other motives for murder besides revenge).[9] It seems that the U.S. Postal Service has received disproportionate, and one should argue, unfair, media attention—and maybe we can now think twice before using the term "going postal."

So, contrary to what many people believe, what we have found in our research is that most cases of workplace revenge are nonviolent (for example, the silent treatment, badmouthing). Why, then, should managers pay attention to this phenomenon, and why should organizations care? Because revenge nevertheless can be harmful, sometimes extremely so, resulting in destroyed careers and worse. This returns us to our point about how revenge can serve as a critical signal to the organization. Revenge does not happen in a vacuum. Revenge happens when formal systems break down, when an organization's mechanisms for preventing or correcting injustice don't work. Or when stupid mistakes go undetected in the system—until someone gets hurt by them. When the formal system proves inadequate, the informal system will step in to handle the problem, for better or worse. In other words, where there's workplace revenge, you can bet the organization is overlooking bad behavior or a dysfunctional process somewhere along the line.

Case in point: an employee decides to enter a part-time, evening MBA program, counting on a company benefits package that promises to reimburse tuition. After enrolling, paying the tuition, and beginning classes, the employee completes the myriad forms and submits the tuition bill for reimbursement, only to find that the company suddenly changed its benefits policy and now won't pay for tuition. Out thousands of dollars, the outraged employee vows to find a new job.

Revenge, then, can serve as a valuable warning bell to companies to sit up and pay attention. In that sense, you can view revenge as a sometimes positive phenomenon. It's a way of restoring justice where justice has broken down, and it can be a potent motivator for constructive change. That revenge can sometimes be positive strikes many people as absurd, in part because they consider only the party who is hurt by revenge. But to fully understand revenge, it is necessary to consider other parties and to account for the positive as well as negative outcomes.

First, who are the parties in the conflict? Whose interests does a revenge act serve and whose interests does it harm? After all, what's good for one party may not be good for another. We know from our research that, in any revenge episode, more than one set of interests is at stake.[10] For example, the episode clearly features an *avenger*, the one seeking revenge in response to the perceived harm caused by an *offender*, who may be another individual or the organization itself; in addition, there are almost always *bystanders*, innocents caught in the wake of the revenge. So at a minimum, at least three different sets of interests can be affected by the act of revenge, and each must be considered when judging the act's consequences.[11]

Second, what kinds of outcomes result from revenge? Yes, we find that revenge can be destructive and antisocial, but it can also lead to *constructive* and *pro-social* outcomes. For example, the avenger may feel vindicated and empowered putting down the offender, but the offender is upset (perhaps even bewildered, not even knowing that an offense has occurred), and innocent bystanders may find the tension awkward, or may benefit from seeing a chronic offender put down. Thus, while revenge typically has bad, ugly faces, it also can have a good face (see following box).

The Case of the Eclipse Team

Sometimes revenge can yield positive results indeed. Take the case of the Eclipse team at Data General in the early 1980s, whose story was made famous by Tracy Kidder's Pulitzer-prize-winning book, *Soul of a New Machine* (1981). A group of engineers were passed over to work on Data General's newest, and most exciting and challenging, computer project—a project that upper management deemed necessary to save the company. A senior manager named Tom West took the demoralized, bitter engineers and challenged them on a different project. In fact, he played off their feelings of resentment, encouraging them to be angry with upper management. In other words, West relied on the revenge motive and channeled the engineers' anger into proving the CEO and other engineers wrong about who were the best engineers in the firm. The result? They built a better computer much faster, and their computer ended up being the one Data General produced and marketed.

The avenging engineers at Data General did not have the most benign, company-oriented motivation. Rather, their primary motivation for working so hard was to regain their reputation. But two points are important here. First, while the avenging engineers may not have judged their own intentions as noble, they believed they were justified. They believed they were, in every sense of the word, good people. Second, regardless of their intentions, their response benefited the company tremendously. Saved it, in fact.

But as we pointed out earlier, it is important to remember that even revenge that results in such a happy outcome is *risky*. Things don't always work out as planned. Remember the saying, "The road to hell is paved with good intentions"? Sometimes what an avenger hopes will be a one-shot act that evens the score escalates into a lengthy feud. Escalation is surprisingly hard to stop once it starts.[12] Moreover, often revenge is just plain bad, and we can't always predict which outcome a desire for revenge will turn into. In fact, even the desire for revenge is in itself an unpleasant thing to experience.

Consider too the dramatic examples where revenge—especially the threat of revenge—has proven extremely useful in promoting cooperation,[13] and where it has served as a powerful constraint against power abuse and injustice in organizations.[14] When people fear revenge, they are more careful not to provoke conflict.[15] For example, during the Cold War, the promise of "Mutually Assured Destruction" or MAD (considered by many to be the best acronym, *ever*) was NATO's and the Warsaw Pact's agreement that if one side launched its nuclear missiles, the other side would retaliate by launching its missiles. Indeed, to make sure the revenge threat remained credible, neither side was allowed to build interceptor missiles for defense. This MAD policy is now widely credited for keeping the two sides from going to war for thirty years (proxy wars not included).

A similar fear in the workplace can keep employees in check: for instance, managers who fear that their most indispensable workers might suddenly quit will be careful not to mistreat them. And as we've already mentioned, the *outcome* of revenge itself sometimes can be positive as well (such as the case of the humiliated manager who "gets even" with the boss by performing better)—although, again, we think even this kind of revenge deserves an organization's attention.

All of this is to say that there may be a different way of looking at revenge than how we've all been accustomed to viewing it. In fact, what we're arguing for in this book is a broader, more value-free view of workplace revenge: that there is something to be gained by learning to identify revenge in all its forms. We think that once managers and organizations understand why and how employees seek revenge, they can learn to predict, manage, and ultimately prevent its ill effects.

After all, managers already spend an inordinate amount of time trying to sort out conflict. One study showed that middle managers spend an average of 25 percent of their time on this effort, while the numbers were even higher for first-line supervisors. This same study found that CEOs spend 26 percent of their time dealing with conflict.[16] Yet most don't usually handle conflict very well. Rather than make peace, too often they ignore or inflame the conflict—fertile ground indeed for the "informal system" of workplace revenge to take over. For example, another study found that subordinates who perceived more conflicts at work also viewed their supervisors as avoiding conflict.[17] Indeed, avoiding conflict may be the most popular approach to conflict, and often the most ineffective in Western cultures.[18]

We've written this book, therefore, for managers, HR executives, and top leaders who want to learn to promote fair behavior in their organizations and curb the damage that workplace revenge often causes. We are also aware that some readers of this book might find themselves at some point feeling an impulse toward revenge *themselves*, or at the very least needing some basic skills to talk down a disgruntled worker so as to prevent efforts to take revenge. We've therefore included a chapter in this book that addresses key things that a revenge-seeker should consider, such as ways to cope with angry feelings and some practical tips for controlling potentially damaging impulses.

An Overview of the Book

Our research into workplace revenge originally grew out of our deep interest in the subject of organizational justice. Specifically, we found that most of the literature on organizational justice had little to say about what employees actually *do* once they perceive that an injustice has occurred. So we set out to see what employees do. One thing many employees do is get even. When we found that many forms of workplace revenge are rather mild and commonplace (rather than violent), we became curious: What motivates an otherwise normal, mild-mannered employee to quietly (or not so quietly) seek revenge? And what forms does this quest for justice take?

As noted, our conclusions are based on fifteen years of our own research on this topic, as well as decades of others' social science research in the psychology of management, organizational justice,[19] social cognition (that is, the study of how people make sense of other people and themselves),[20] aggression,[21] forgiveness,[22] and social deviance.[23] Through all this research, we have looked through the keyhole in the corporate door, peering at hundreds of conflicts, and have come up with a few surprising findings (see following box).

Seven Things About Revenge That Might Surprise You

☐ *Revenge has little to do with the avenger's personality.* At least, not as much as you'd think. The biggest predictor of whether employees act on a revenge impulse is not their personalities but rather the *actions of their manager or coworkers.* In short, managers wishing to prevent revenge should not worry so much about what kind of employees they have; they should worry about how those employees are treated.

☐ *More employees than you'd think are vigilantes-in-waiting.* Overall, what we find is that most revenge is committed by normal, well-meaning people who are simply trying to right a wrong. In their minds, they are pursuing *justice*. If the authorities in the organization won't handle an offense, and if workers believe they can get away with revenge, then many normal employees will take the law into their own hands and seek to get even.

☐ *When it comes to justice, employees think just like citizens and juries think.* The justice principles that citizens use to judge the fairness of laws and their enforcement turn out to be the same principles that employees use in the workplace. That is, people care that troublemakers get the outcomes they deserve (for example, prison sentence, disciplinary action), from processes that are consistently and objectively applied, and that they are treated with dignity and respect throughout the process. Violations of these principles in the workplace anger employees, sometimes enough to take the law into their own hands.

☐ *Avengers (and often observers) view revenge as a moral and rational act.* At the moment avengers seek revenge, they often have reasoned out that revenge is appropriate and morally justified. They believe that revenge is the right thing to do. And not just avengers think this, but often so do observers, who vicariously experience that feeling of righteousness when others are harmed or when a harm-doer is dealt swift vengeance.[24] In specific circumstances, then, officemates will tolerate revenge.

□ *Revenge is rarely served cold.* Despite the proverb, "Revenge is a dish best served cold,"* avengers rarely follow this advice. Although revenge is rational, it also is heated. Avengers often act out of anger. We don't mean chronically angry people who explode at the slightest inconvenience, but normal people who feel shock and outrage. Revenge arises from *righteous anger*, a set of emotions that have a moral foundation, reflecting a sense of violation. These emotions can be intense and long-lasting, and they often fuel the obsession to get even. Perhaps worse, the combination of simmering anger and obsession leads to bad decisions. Instincts do not always make for better decision making, especially when the situation is complex.

□ *Avengers often blame inaccurately.* Common wisdom has it that a victim of a perceived wrongdoing should not be allowed to serve as judge, jury, and executioner, in part because victims often blame the wrong person, or blame the right person too harshly. The same applies to avengers in the workplace.

□ *Revenge can be creative, but so can the alternatives.* Avenging employees may do something relatively mild, such as construct elaborate revenge fantasies that they have no intention of acting upon, or more extremely, they may bad-mouth the offender, lodge a complaint, sabotage performance, or sue someone. But many angry workers simply do nothing, while others forgive or attempt reconciliation.

---

*The original source of this proverb is disputed. We honestly don't know where it came from. Some attribute it to the revenge-obsessed Shakespeare, but not to a specific play. We consulted Shakespeare scholar Michael Delahoyd, who says it's not from Shakespeare. Some attribute it to Pierre Choderlos de Leaclos, from 1782, in *Les Liaisons dangereuses*, but others claim it is not in the original French text. It was certainly uttered in the movie, *Star Trek II: Wrath of Khan*, which is why some people refer to it as a Klingon proverb (as in the movie *Kill Bill: Vol. 1*), but this is unlikely to have been where it was first used.

Throughout this book, we will unravel the complexities of these findings in the most interesting and useful way we can. As you read, we ask you to keep an open mind about workplace revenge. To better understand revenge, to understand why the workers we studied acted on it, we had to be willing to see the conflict from their point of view. For managers to prevent workplace revenge, they need to see the conflict from the employees' perspective, and not just fall back on the more familiar managerial perspective. Thus managers must fathom why an employee—and a normal, nice, sane employee at that—would think that revenge might be a great answer to a current problem. Managers who cannot adopt this perspective will have a much harder time seeing it coming. And if you can't see it coming, it's harder to stop it.

To summarize, the focus of our book is on explaining the social and psychological causes of revenge in the workplace. In particular, we argue that *the motivation for revenge is primarily rooted in the sense of injustice.* Further, *revenge should be seen as actions intended to restore a sense of justice.* The following chapters provide greater insight into predicting and preventing revenge in the workplace.

In Chapter Two, we expand on our theory of revenge in the workplace; that is, our core premise that most employees who seek revenge are motivated out of a sense of injustice. They therefore are seeking some form of justice, either from the organization or by their own hands. The theory is simply that offenses are seen as provocations, which lead to blaming, which leads to anger and a desire for revenge, which often lead to acts of revenge. In some cases, people just live with the anger and do nothing in response. And in other cases, the anger and desire for revenge are transformed into forgiveness and reconciliation. Which behavior anger and the desire for revenge lead to depends on the amount of power the victim has, the climate of fairness in the organization, and the victim's personality.

While Chapter Two gives an overview of our theory as a whole, Chapters Three to Six drill down into each part of our theory. Thus, to begin, Chapter Three explores in detail the three kinds of workplace offenses that trigger revenge: goal obstruction, breaking the rules and social norms, and damage to reputation—offering many examples of each kind of trigger.

Chapter Four gets inside the mind of the person who is contemplating revenge. Specifically, once provoked, people want to know why the provocation occurred—and who is to blame. Blame is the lynchpin to motivating revenge. In this chapter, we explore psychological and social factors that shape, and often skew, the blame assignment process.

But revenge is shaped not only by the assignment of blame. In Chapter Five, we explore how the desire for revenge is grounded in a righteous anger, an anger that has a moral foundation demanding justice. This righteous anger is a set of emotions that also shape one's thinking about the acts of revenge.

Chapter Six focuses on whether and how people act out their righteous anger. Whether revenge occurs depends on several questions that victims often ask themselves. In particular, victims ask, "If I don't get even, will justice be served some other way?" Next, they ask, "Do I have the power to get away with revenge, without inviting counterretaliation?" Answers to these questions influence the victims' thoughts and emotions about how to act out their righteous anger. Also, we discuss personality differences: some people can be pushed past the breaking point easily; others can't.

In Chapter Seven, we offer practical advice for leaders who must deal with angry employees and would-be avengers. First, it is our position that it is the responsibility of leaders to actively and regularly assess the social and emotional undercurrents that give rise to revenge. Second, leaders must understand the conflict from the victim's point of view. Unless leaders deal with the root cause or provocation, the conflict may not end, but merely be postponed. Third, leaders must act quickly, before the victim's obsession turns to revenge. Fourth, organizations should attempt informal mediation between the victim and offender. Finally, should mediation fail, leaders need to ensure that the offender is punished if in fact an offense has been committed. Through these steps, leaders are administering justice so that victims do not engage in their own form of vigilante justice.

Another way to stop revenge is for the would-be avengers themselves to consider the consequences and understand the alternatives. Our theory leads to advice for them, as well. Thus, in Chapter Seven we also speak directly to victims of workplace offenses and offer practical advice as how to *avoid* revenge, as often the costs outweigh the benefits. Specifically, we offer ten considerations designed to discourage revenge, which we call "Counting to 10." In particular, we focus on

- How to more accurately view one's situation
- How to constructively manage one's anger
- How to resolve conflict situations before they trigger an act of revenge or escalate into a feud

In the concluding chapter of the book, Chapter Eight, we connect workplace peace to workplace justice. What everyone—from the lowest-level employee to the highest-level manager—wants is peace. Revenge and related conflict can be gut-wrenching, distracting, and usually unproductive. Peace without justice, however, is tyranny—and it does not last. Lasting peace, we argue, requires a sequencing of virtues. Specifically, peace requires reconciliation; reconciliation is easier after forgiveness; and forgiveness occurs more easily after justice has been served. The bottom line? Managers wishing to prevent workplace revenge should worry less about which of their employees may be vengeful and worry more about how fairly they treat their employees. And if they treat their employees fairly, it will lead to a more productive workplace.[25]

With that overview, let us now turn to Chapter Two and a detailed look at our theory of revenge. This model, grounded in empirical research findings, underpins the practical advice we offer later in Chapter Seven.

2

PEERING INTO THE SOUL OF DISCONTENT

The Phenomenon of Revenge

Revenge is an act of passion; vengeance of justice.
Injuries are revenged; crimes are avenged

—*Samuel Johnson*

Former Oracle senior vice president Terry Garnett does not mince words. "I do hold grudges," Garnett says. "Am I motivated by that? Absolutely."[1] Garnett was referring specifically to a grudge he has long held against his old boss and Oracle CEO and co-founder Larry Ellison. In the early 1990s Garnett traveled the world with Ellison as the company attempted to start up an interactive-TV business. When Ellison invited Garnett and his wife to accompany him on a vacation to Kyoto in 1994, Garnett took it as a confirmation of his and Ellison's deepening trust and friendship. As Jena McGregor described the trip in a 2007 cover story in *Business Week:* "That year marked the 1,200th anniversary of the founding of Japan's former imperial capital, a meaningful occasion for Ellison, a passionate Japanophile. Together, he, Garnett, and four others made the pilgrimage along the cherry-blossom-lined Philosopher's Walk to the famed Ginkakuji Temple."[2]

But just weeks after their return from that trip, Ellison called Garnett into his office and informed him that he had canned the interactive-TV project. What was more, Garnett was fired—and

Ellison offered no clear reason, Garnett claims. "It was pretty clinical," he recalls. "I tried to keep composed." Stunned, Garnett packed up his office and left the building, but he later sued Ellison for firing him without just cause. Oracle's reply to Garnett's suit cited his "declining productivity." Although Garnett dropped the lawsuit, he promised himself he'd get even. Today, as CEO of the software start-up Ingres Corp., Garnett may get his chance as his company works overtime to shuffle market share away from Oracle.[3]

But revenge of course is not the sole province of leaders in the boardroom; it occurs at all levels of the organization. Consider the story of a telecommunications executive we talked to whose company was in the midst of a merger with another company. In an effort to build bridges, as he put it, he decided to reach out to one of his new colleagues, knowing that "even though we were from 'different' organizations, we had to work together to succeed in this new company." He shared personal confidences and inside information on the company workings, all with the intention of getting his colleague off to a running start. But his new officemate either misinterpreted or intentionally misrepresented what he was told. "He used that information to suggest to people that I was betraying confidences to get ahead," said the executive. "That couldn't be farther from the truth. I was trying to *help* him. I vowed from that moment on that I would do everything in my power to bring him down."

What is revenge all about? What pushes nice, ordinary folks like these past the breaking point, leading them to desire revenge and even to act it out? These are questions that have fascinated human beings since the story of Cain and Abel was first recounted. And for us, over the past fifteen years, they have captured our imagination and energy. In this chapter, we outline our model, which we believe illuminates some answers to these questions. We begin with two beliefs we've uncovered about how and why the phenomenon of revenge happens in the first place.

The Underlying Sources of Revenge:
Two Perspectives

Our search for answers has led us to two very different perspectives as to why revenge occurs in the workplace: the manager-centered perspective and the employee-centered perspective. The *manager-centered perspective* views revenge primarily through the eyes and interests of the organization and its managers,[4] and it demands that the answer should focus on employees' personalities. That is, in answering the question "what pushes people past the breaking point?" it focuses on where employees' *breaking points* are to be found. According to this perspective, some people break more easily: some are just more fragile, volatile, aggressive, impulsive, or easily offended than others. This perspective suggests that to prevent workplace revenge, examine which employees are more vengeful. Perhaps such vengeful and fragile employees could be monitored more closely, reformed, or even better yet, never hired in the first place.

Conveniently, this belief places the blame for revenge squarely on the employee. Revenge is the fault of the avenger. It is a bad act, committed by bad employees—employees who are unprofessional, mean-spirited, and overly emotional. Were they not this way, vengeance would not happen. Following from these premises, managers focus on developing strategies and what they think of as solutions to control, if not eliminate, anger and discontent in the workplace. Such strategies can range from implementing different employee selection procedures to increasing surveillance of employees to terminating employees thought to be likely to engage in revenge.[5] While these managerial strategies and solutions may somewhat reduce anger and rage, they certainly won't eliminate them. In fact, monitoring can backfire when angry people get even with the supervisors who institute monitoring policies.[6]

The *employee-centered perspective*, on the other hand, focuses on the situational events that trigger anger and revenge. This perspective asks what *pushes* employees past the breaking point. In other words, what forces are doing the pushing? According to this perspective, it is provocations by others at work that drive employees to act. Were it not for these offenses, harms, and slights, employees would have nothing to avenge. If managers and coworkers did not mistreat their direct reports and colleagues, there would be no workplace revenge.

Moreover, the harmed individuals interpret an *act of injustice* as the situation that triggers anger and rage. This interpretation provides employees with the moral justification for revenge, which is why avengers believe they are doing the right thing, or doing justice. This type of justification is not too surprising, once one remembers that few people in the world see their own acts of incivility, deviance, disobedience, and even violence as indicators of being evil. That is, regardless of what others think of their actions, people rarely see themselves as evil.[7] At the time they make choices that the majority regards as unethical, they believe they are doing good.[8] (But read the following box.)

The Case of the Micromanager

An organization with a culture of delegation and chain of command once hired a manager who could not resist micromanaging.[9] No matter how small the detail, he demanded that his direct reports seek his approval before making a decision. Worse, he often went around his direct reports without informing them, violating the chain of command, telling their subordinates what to do. Three of his direct reports finally decided they'd had enough and plotted to teach him a lesson so that they could regain their autonomy. These employees supervised the same department, but each covered a different eight-hour shift; collectively, they covered the twenty-four-hour day.

Their strategy? They decided to give their boss exactly what he wanted, sort of: they called him in on every minor emergency, no matter what time of day or night. As their vengeance progressed, they deprived their boss of sleep. This strategy was so effective that their boss soon suffered a nervous breakdown, which effectively ended his career.

These employees did not believe they were doing the wrong thing when they hatched their plot. On the contrary, they believed that by discouraging the boss's counternormative and unproductive micromanaging, they were not only restoring justice but also improving workplace productivity. They had no idea the boss's health would suffer.

Hindsight can indicate that their plot was unnecessarily hurtful, serving as the kind of example that gives revenge a bad name. But our points are these: at the time, they thought the revenge would make everybody better off, and the petty tyranny of the manager must be counted as a triggering cause of the events that unfolded.

Less conveniently, the employee-centered perspective places the blame for revenge squarely on the provocateurs, and often on management. In other words, it is the provocations that *push* normal individuals to commit extreme acts. According to this perspective, the focus of attention should be on environmental triggers of workplace aggression.

We believe that *both* the employee-centered and manager-centered perspectives are correct. Like most psychologists, we believe that most social behavior is caused not by the situation or by the personality, but by both working together. While this may seem obvious, we are frequently amazed at how many managers focus only on the personality aspect. When we speak publicly on workplace revenge, someone in the audience always asks us which personality tests will best help them weed out vindictive employees. Of course, at the same public talks, some people in the audience always approach us afterward to share their stories of a time they got even. Interestingly, they focus only on the situation.

We have much more to say in upcoming chapters about the competing perspectives of situation and personality, and how such competing perspectives escalate conflicts. For now, we emphasize two points. First, any theory of revenge must account for both perspectives—and indeed our research has confirmed this. Second, in terms of workplace revenge, the situational factors (the focus of the employee perspective) are a much more powerful predictor of revenge than are the personality factors.

How do we know this? We've interviewed and surveyed real managers about their experiences with revenge, and we have conducted a dozen empirical studies, including interviewing more than five hundred employees about nearly eight hundred incidents of workplace revenge, surveying corporate and government employees, and conducting experiments. We've measured patterns, and we've compiled these patterns into a model of what avengers do, how they do it, and why they do it. Also, each piece of the model has been tested by anywhere from dozens to hundreds of other scholars in such fields as the psychology of organizational justice, criminal justice, social cognition (that is, the study of how people make sense of other people and themselves), game theory, power and influence, conflict resolution, negotiation, forgiveness, motivation, leadership, communications, and consumer behavior. Moreover, because we tested our model in a variety of contexts (such as government agencies and for-profit firms, with low-level employees and with executives as well as college students), we've learned that it applies to many kinds of employees in different industries, and in a variety of workplace situations.

The Core of Workplace Revenge:
Let Justice Be Done

At the core of our model lies a simple assertion: employees need to see their workplaces as fair, and therefore when they perceive acts of unfairness, they need to see justice restored. (See Figure 2.1.) Victims want to see offenders punished, and possibly to get back whatever the offenders took away from them, whether it be their money, their sense of "law and order" in the organization, or even

Figure 2.1 Our Model of Revenge

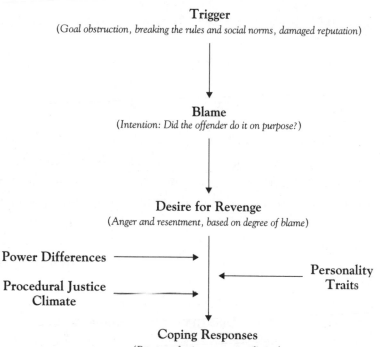

Trigger
(*Goal obstruction, breaking the rules and social norms, damaged reputation*)

Blame
(*Intention: Did the offender do it on purpose?*)

Desire for Revenge
(*Anger and resentment, based on degree of blame*)

Power Differences

Procedural Justice Climate

Personality Traits

Coping Responses
(*Revenge, forgiveness, reconciliation*)

Note: Which coping response the last downward arrow points to—revenge, forgiveness, or reconciliation—is affected by the sideways arrows, which push and pull the downward arrow toward one response or another.

their reputation. But if such justice is served by the organization or by the offender, there is no rational need for the victim to seek justice through revenge.

What, then, do employees do when they believe that justice will *not* be restored by organizational authorities? In these cases, many victim-employees are potential vigilantes who will pursue justice on their own if the conditions are right. If employees have the means, and if they believe justice won't be restored any other way, they are more likely to seek to restore justice themselves—by their own hands—that is, by revenge or getting even. Specifically, employees are more likely to get even in response to workplace offenses when two conditions exist:

- They have the power to get even, as indicated by their rank within the organization.
- They also perceive that the organization generally does not use fair procedures, which leads them to believe that organizational authorities will not punish offenders.

In our model, the conflict begins when an offender somehow harms, mistreats, insults, or generally offends the victim. This offense is the *trigger* of revenge. Three main triggers we've identified include goal obstruction, in which someone gets blocked somehow in their pursuit of some job or career objective; breaking the rules and social norms (such as arbitrary application of rules and standards, lying); and damage to reputation (such as backbiting attacks or interpersonal indignities).[10]

Next, the victim analyzes the offense. This analysis is at the core of what we call *the blame game*. For example, people evaluate the pain and hurt, and ask why the offender did it. The greater the suspected intentionality of the offender's motivation is (that is, the more the victim thinks the offender offended *on purpose*), then the more the victim blames the offender. Next, the greater the blame, the greater the anger and resentment—and the more often and more seriously the victim *desires* to get even.

The victim then decides how to deal or cope with the desire for revenge by choosing a course of action. Alternative courses of action include revenge, forgiveness, and reconciliation. Which response the victim chooses depends directly on the strength of the desire for revenge: the higher the desire, the more likely the victim chooses revenge over forgiveness or reconciliation, or both.

But the coping response the victim chooses is also constrained or encouraged by many other factors, such as opportunity for revenge, closeness of relationship between victim and offender, power, organizational norms, personality traits, and gender, to name but a few. We focus on three factors that we have investigated ourselves and that have been studied by other social scientists exploring the psychology of workplace justice.

The first factor is *social power*. The more power the victim has relative to the offender, the more means the victim has for getting even; and, the more means available, the more likely one of those means will be used. Second is the *climate at work regarding fairness*. Specifically, do employees believe that management has fair procedures and applies them consistently? The fairer the climate, the more likely a victim will use official grievance channels (for example, consulting an organizational ombudsperson or entering a respected manager's open door) rather than get even by private means. The third and last factor in our model is *personality traits*. After all, not all victims of similar offenses in similar situations respond the same way. Some people are naturally more forgiving than others.

Revenge as an Act of Justice

We came upon the phenomenon of revenge-as-justice-seeking when we began our research over fifteen years ago. When we asked executives and working professionals if they ever engaged in acts of revenge in the workplace, most responded with an emphatic "No!" And we found that, in general, acts of revenge or even discussion of revenge in the workplace were treated as taboo.[11] But when we phrased the question differently—for example, "Do you ever try to *get even* with others at work?"—the response was almost always "Of course, all the time!" Such confessions were usually followed by an enthusiastic recounting of the events. ("Let me tell you about this one jerk I got even with....")

The fact that people say they do not engage in revenge, but they do try to get even, confirms our finding that what attracts people to revenge (whether called by that name or not) is that it is considered a righteous and just act. Witness the audience's applause and approval of acts of revenge in such films as *Dirty Harry* and *The First Wives Club,* or in our continued fascination with the story of Medea, whose revenge destroyed her selfish ex-husband (and unfortunately her children as well). For that matter, consider that most of Shakespeare's plays contain revenge plots. As Shylock says in *The Merchant of Venice,* "And if you wrong us, shall we not want revenge?" In fact, don't most action movies build in a revenge plot as part of the story line?

Historically, the concept of revenge has been inextricably linked with the concept of justice to the point that revenge and justice were once nearly synonymous.[12] But as civilizations evolved, revenge became decoupled from justice as the state took over the authority for revenge, to maintain civic order.[13] Those who engaged in revenge, then, were not engaging in justice itself but rather in *wild* justice. "The proper relationship between justice and revenge has been a major preoccupation of literature, religion, and law throughout the recorded history of the West," observed Susan Jacoby, in her 1983 book (titled *Wild Justice*). "Establishment of a balance between the restraint that enables people to live with one another and the ineradicable impulse to retaliate when harm is inflicted has always been one of the essential tasks of civilization."[14] While this has become the conventional wisdom on revenge, our research finds that most people still view their efforts at revenge as acts of justice.

Indeed, revenge has been described to us as action motivated to restore justice.

Not only do people justify their acts of revenge as morally right, they view their actions as rational responses to what happened to them. For instance, while engaging in revenge, people reported their strong belief that they were "doing the right thing" and that they were "doing justice."[15] Thus, while the act of revenge may have served self-interest, it often serves other interests, and it is usually justified in moral terms.[16] (We examine this more closely in Chapter Five, where we explore the concept of "righteous anger.") The justice rationale can be a powerful motivation and justification for revenge (see following box).

The Case of the Avenging Report-Writer

One of the executives in our study had a boss who always took credit for ideas that she had developed. This boss would "empower" the executive to do the research and write up the results and recommendations on a specific business strategy or issue. But each time the report was then presented to senior leadership in the firm, it had a new title page in which the boss put his name and deleted the executive's name. When questions arose from senior leadership about the report, the boss would "defer" to the executive and let her answer the questions, thus looking good to his superiors for empowering his subordinate.

After this occurred twice within a year, the executive decided "No more!" Two months later, her research was to be presented at another senior leadership meeting. Like clockwork, the boss put his name on the title page and deleted hers. But this time, she called in sick to the meeting. When the senior leadership began to ask questions, the boss had no one to bail him out. Curious as to why the boss was so ignorant of a report he had supposedly written, the senior leadership launched an investigation that ultimately led to the boss's dismissal. The final point of this poetic justice? The executive who was denied credit for her ideas was promoted into her boss's job. Indeed, in this case, revenge was sweet!

The Three Triggers of Revenge

What exactly is it that avengers and forgivers are avenging or forgiving? How does a victim evaluate the offense and decide on an action? In other words, how does the nature of the offense influence which response the victim chooses?

As we've said, we find three categories of workplace offense against which victims consider retaliating: goal obstruction, breaking the rules and social norms, and damage to reputation.

Goal Obstruction. Goal obstruction occurs when a coworker's actions thwart an employee from reaching a goal. An example of goal obstruction is a coworker who wins a promotion, thus thwarting another employee's achievement of that same promotion. Also, when supervisors give their direct reports ambitious goals but take away the resources needed to achieve those goals, employees become angry. Goal obstruction can lead to frustration, and the experience of frustration can lead people to take revenge.

For example, a middle manager in a U.S. federal agency tells the following story: "Our agency has just been reorganized into a new division and a decision will be made in the next few months as to who will be the head of that division. My superior wants the job and so do I. She knows that and wants to make me look bad. So she has been giving me all the "inexperienced" people to work with, hoping to see me fail, thus ensuring her promotion.

But I *don't* fail, which only makes her more mad and motivated to find new ways to torpedo me."

Breaking the Rules and Social Norms. Employees are motivated to seek revenge when others do things the culture defines as improper. An example is an executive who promotes someone who does not meet the rules and criteria for promotion. Generally, violating the rules is perceived as unfair. Also, if an employer makes written promises about a future salary and bonus structure for an employee but breaks those promises, then that breach of contract may motivate the employee to get even through a grievance or a lawsuit. Such violations are not limited to formal rules and contracts; they also include breaches of informal social norms, etiquette, and promises. Examples of breaking social norms include bosses or coworkers who shirk their job responsibilities, take undue credit for a team's performance, or outright steal ideas.

Norms are also violated when private confidences or secrets are disclosed to others inside or outside the organization—that is, when people feel betrayed by someone they trusted, particularly if the betrayal is premeditated and intentional. Lying, in particular, upsets employees. In general, if employees come to feel that managers' and coworkers' words and intentions cannot be counted on, if the rules don't really exist, then their sense that the workplace has order weakens and they feel that they are one step closer to chaos. To avoid this fate, some employees step in to enforce the rules and promises themselves.

Damage to Reputation. Attempts to tarnish a person's reputation can also motivate revenge. For example, destructive criticism, public ridicule intended to embarrass a subordinate or coworker, and false accusations by a boss or peer can trigger revenge. Beyond intentional put-downs, unintentional acts on the part of bosses who are hypercritical, overdemanding, and overly harsh—even cruel—in their dealings with subordinates over time can provoke revenge.

And this category is not purely a matter of attacks on reputation; it's also about attacks on status. People who perceive themselves to be of higher status, by virtue of job title or expertise, expect to be treated accordingly. If such high-status people perceive themselves to be disrespected—that is, "dissed"—they may try to restore their status by getting even. Listen to the words of a financial services executive describing his reaction to another executive whom he felt had disrespected him: "I am a vice-president, next in line for promotion to senior vice-president. Some new 'hot-shot' they just hired decided to 'score' some points at my expense at a meeting of senior management. He may have won the battle that day, but he lost the war. Over the next several weeks I bad-mouthed this hot-shot to everybody who would listen. In the end, the hot-shot got all the 'crap' projects and never got promoted."

Blame and the Desire for Revenge

A victim who notices the harm next assesses the offender's acts and motives to determine how to respond. Much like a prosecutor considering why a criminal committed a crime, victim-employees investigate their offending coworkers to determine an appropriate sentence. Blame is important to victims: how much should the offender be blamed? That depends: did the offender *intend* to cause harm? If the victim judges that the offender did not intend to cause the harm but was merely negligent, then the victim blames the offender only a little. If the victim instead judges that the offender caused the harm on purpose, then the victim blames the offender a lot. And there are shades of "on purpose" that matter. Just as judges usually award harsher sentences for premeditated murders than for spontaneous crimes of passion, employees are more motivated to get even with offenders who pick their victim for personal and malicious reasons (say, the offender hates a particular person and wants to see that person suffer) than for impersonal or opportunistic reasons (that is, the offender had nothing against the particular victim; it's just that the victim was in the way or in the wrong place at the wrong time). In the end, the stronger the blame, the stronger the revenge. After all, employees, just like judges and juries, have a sense of proportion that the punishment should fit the crime.

Unfortunately, the punishment does not always fit the crime. Why? Because, unlike the people who carry out the work of the legal system, employees . . .

Investigate what they view as crimes partially, resulting in. . .

An incomplete, biased, and distorted collection of evidence, which is then weighed by. . .

An angry victim with neither the training nor the detachment of a formal judge and jury, who then may. . .

Attempt to administer justice personally, even without having the best means to do so.

The result of this biased, error-prone process is that the victim will assign more blame to the offender than more objective third parties would agree the offender deserves. Such biases and overascribed blame are what make revenge such a *sloppy* form of justice. It is precisely this biased sloppiness that gives vigilantism its deservedly bad name. That is, a procedurally fair, formalized adjudication of offenses is a form of justice restoration superior to vigilantism. This process minimizes and counterbalances the ego-defensive biases of victims, thus usually leading to fairer verdicts and punishments and keeping innocent people from getting lynched.

Regrettably, too many organizations do not use a procedurally fair, formalized adjudication of offenses, and thus end up with too many vigilantes—employees who each feel they must restore justice by serving as their own judge, jury, and executioner, as well as their own detective and district attorney. This is unfortunate because victims are just as awful at playing judge, jury, detective, and the rest in the workplace as they were in the old Wild West, and too often blame inaccurately.[17]

The resulting tragedy is a familiar theme in fiction. For instance, in the 1943 movie, *The Ox-Bow Incident*, citizens of a town took the law into their own hands and hanged three people they thought had killed a popular rancher, Larry Kincaid, after stealing his cattle. When the sheriff arrived just after the hanging, he informed the town citizens that Larry Kincaid was still alive and that he had just arrested the people responsible for stealing the cattle. Similarly, in the 2003 movie, *Mystic River*, Jimmy Markum's daughter is killed, in response to which Jimmy launches his own informal investigation through his own neighborhood friends. His investigation leads him to his childhood friend, Dave Boyle, as the likely suspect. So, Jimmy stabs and shoots Dave, dumping his body in the Mystic River, only to discover the next morning that the police have arrested the real killers.

When coworkers are blamed incorrectly or too harshly for provocations, fortunately we don't see hangings and shootouts—but we do see things like rude comments, unhelpful attitudes, and missing office supplies. What's really interesting, and useful for managers trying to prevent revenge, are the predictable ways in which workplace victims blame inaccurately. Victims play mental tricks on themselves, some of which are tinged with paranoia. For instance, victims are prone to see motives to harm that aren't really there: they often see intention or conspiracies where none exist. This justice-centered, sense-making, obsessive process can make angry victims even angrier.[18]

Consider the following example of a financial services executive who believed he was being left out of a key meeting by a peer, thus motivating an act of revenge. This executive had been identified as a high-potential leader with a bright future. It happened that senior management had invited all high-potential leaders to a major meeting, except for him. One of this executive's so-called friends told him that he was left out of the meeting because one of the other high-potential leaders, who was responsible for managing the meeting, intentionally excluded him in order to get ahead. Outraged, the executive vowed to get even with his peer. When the meeting began, this executive entered the room and interrupted senior management by bad-mouthing the peer. After this emotional tirade, senior management asked him to leave, and the executive was terminated days later. It turns out that the executive had *in fact* been invited by his peer, but the invitation had been lost in the ether because of an e-mail server problem. The failure to do his due diligence and correctly determine what had happened led this executive to falsely blame his peer, which cost the executive his job.

So what we see, then, is that although revenge may be a dish best served cold, it is usually cooked in a very hot kitchen. Employees who try to get even are people who are (or were) really angry. (For a good example of how emotions can drive revenge, see the following box.) When we interviewed employees about revenge, the interviewees often focused on the intensity of their emotions. For example, the initial emotions of injustice are often described as quite hot and volatile, characterized by expressions of pain, anger, and rage. In describing these emotions, people use such words as "furious" and "bitter," and describe how they felt engulfed in "white-hot" emotions. One person spoke of being "inflamed" and "enraged," "consumed" by thoughts of revenge, while another needed to satisfy the "burning desire of revenge."

The Case of the Envious Executive

An executive in a consumer products company became angry with a program manager in his organization, someone the executive believed was getting too much positive attention and recognition for a track record of successful new product launches. For almost a year, the executive's anger simmered until it finally boiled over. When the time came to reappoint the program manager, the executive got even. Rather than rewarding him for a job well done, the executive cut the program manager's compensation while demanding that the manager do even more in terms of new products! The program manager declined the offer, and left the position. As a result, the program suffered revenue losses approaching $900,000.

The intensity of this desire grew as people engaged in *revenge fantasies*. In vivid and sometimes violent dream scenarios, people would imagine ways to get even with the offender. Such dreams were filled with rich detail, so much so that one could almost feel the pain inflicted by the victim in the act of revenge. One manager described her revenge dream in the following manner:

> The frail old man's eyes bulged and his face contorted wildly as he struggled to free his bound arms and legs. Duct tape covered his mouth....My body trembled in anticipation as I lifted the fifty-pound vat over his writhing body. The golden liquid languorously oozed downward. The rich smell of nectar filled the room. Next came the jar. I placed it in front of his face and carefully unscrewed the lid. I had worked for weeks gathering my little helpers. His frail, honey-covered body stiffened and his eyes widened in horror . . . . "You never should have provoked me," I said with a rueful smile as I headed for the door.

Fantasies like this can fuel the desire for revenge beyond what otherwise might have been a more benign response.[19] In particular, we found that fantasies can fuel revenge when the harm is personal (that is, an attack on one's identity) and people perceive that harm to be intentional, if not malicious.*

---

*As we discuss in Chapter Six, it was more often the case that we found that fantasies lessened the desire for revenge.

In those situations, we found that the desire for revenge was not only heated but also long-lasting. That is, victims often obsessed on their offenders and on the variety of ways to get even. Indeed, the anger over injustice can endure over time, sometimes for days, even weeks and months, if not longer, and thus keep the desire for revenge alive. Chris Matthews, in his 1988 book, *Hardball*, tells the story of one political player who plotted revenge for *eight years*. Of course, the politician later regretted it, if for no other reason than that the offender "lived rent-free inside my head for eight years."[20]

So what do avenging employees actually *do?* Read on.

Choosing a Course of Action: Some Forms of Revenge—And Its Alternatives

While we've never met anyone who accidentally put rat poison instead of creamer in the boss's coffee (as was the story line in the movie 9 *to* 5, with Dolly Parton and Lily Tomlin), we have met hundreds of people who have confessed (and even bragged) about how they evened the score. Sometimes the acts are small and mild; other times they are large and dramatic. Indeed, we have met people who have intentionally destroyed others' careers. But as we described in Chapter One, the great majority of vengeful acts we've found and studied have been mild.

What do we see? Here are a few of the most common forms of revenge:

• *Freeze-Out.* A very popular form of revenge is cooling off social interactions with one's offender. That is, two coworkers may be work buddies who not only work side by side but also socialize at work and outside work. When one offends the other, the offended coworker stops socializing as a form of punishment. Often the punishment is temporary, as the victim gets over it, or feels the point has been made. Sometimes, however, the suspension of socializing is permanent. These work buddies may have gone out for beer after work, asked about each other's families, and so on—but no more. Sure, they still work together, especially if they pride themselves on their professionalism; they just don't socialize anymore.

• *Private Confrontation*. The victim confronts the offender at work, behind closed doors, and "really lets 'em have it." The victim says something along the lines of, "What you did was ethically wrong, and it hurt me; I want it to stop and never happen again." Now, is that really revenge, or is it just correcting a problem behavior? It is revenge if the victims are—whatever their other intentions—trying to shame their offenders, hoping that the offenders feel bad while being scolded. Sometimes, such confrontations occur in public, in front of an audience of other employees. The effect here, if not the goal, is not only to shame the offender but also to publicly embarrass the offender, perhaps while (hopefully) reclaiming one's own status and reputation by showing that the offender is the real villain.

• *Bad-Mouthing*. This is always a possible response if confrontation is not possible or wise. If you don't have the nerve (or foolishness) to tell off the offender face to face, you can always tell your coworkers what a jerk the offender is. Sometimes employees gather socially to share bad-mouthing of coworkers and common bosses.

• *Refusal of Help*. Some victims simply refuse to help the offender. These people believe that overt revenge plots are morally wrong—because one should do no harm—yet they still believe in the norm of reciprocity. So when the offender comes looking for a favor, the victim refuses to grant it. For instance, when an offender later asks a victim for help, the victim refuses, or helps half-heartedly in a passive-aggressive manner. Such victims won't commit misdeeds, but they will omit good deeds. There are many places to draw the line.

• *Quitting*. Perhaps the ultimate act of withholding help is to quit one's job. Scores of people we interviewed talked about quitting as an act of revenge. They say that quitting was not only about getting themselves out of a bad situation, it was about teaching their employer a lesson. The lesson may be "if you treat employees this way, you don't get to keep them." Often, the lesson was "I'll show I'm not worthless by making you do without me; you'll appreciate me after I'm gone, but then it will be too late for you." To pour on the retribution, many who quit did so without giving notice and at the worst possible time, during the heaviest shifts or seasons. For example, people who work in restaurants can quit at 5 PM on Friday night. People who work in U.S. tax preparation firms can quit on April 1.

• *Poor Performance Appraisals*. For people who hold positions of power, the pool of revenge opportunities widens. Bosses can get even with subordinates at their official performance appraisals, giving unusually harsh marks. Unfortunately, we've also heard of cases in our own profession, where professors have given low grades to students who have offended them.

Obviously, the stronger the desire for revenge, the more likely the victim will act on that desire by getting even. But not always.

We've encountered many examples of people seeking alternatives to revenge. First, many victims *forgive* their offenders. They decide that it's best to let go of resentment and their perceived right to get even. Some people simply believe in forgiveness as a dominant moral principle. Some victims can come to understand their offenders and sympathize with their predicament and choices. Other victims simply believe it's in their own best interests to avoid psychological costs of holding a grudge, that the sweet taste of just desserts does not fully compensate for the sustained anger and the obsession that takes over their life of the mind. Surely, there are more pleasant fantasies than revenge fantasies.

Second, many victims *reconcile* with their offenders. Rather than escalate a conflict that (further) damages their relationship, they instead negotiate with the offender, or somehow come to understand the offender better. Note that reconciliation often happens without forgiveness. Some victims work on getting along with their offenders without ever completely letting go of the resentment. This is more likely when the offender is the victim's boss. For example, as one of our interview subjects put it, "I needed his recommendation for my promotion. I was not going to do anything to jeopardize that. I was angry, not stupid." Subordinates usually cannot afford to go to war with their bosses, simply because bosses usually have more power to win such wars. So subordinates reconcile, get along, and hide their true feelings.

Recent research is now beginning to determine more about which angry victims choose which response.[21] As noted earlier, the choice is not simply a matter of the victim's personality or morals; again, it's more of a matter of what kind of organization the victim works for.

Consider the following two examples. A young executive in a consumer products company with a corporate culture known for cutthroat politics observes his boss continually engaging in revenge against his boss's peers—bad-mouthing them, leaving their names off memos, and similar ploys. The boss gets promoted. Now, when faced with what to do in similar situations, the young executive goes to similar tactics of revenge as the first response in dealing with the politics of this company. A second executive in another company observes his boss always trying to engage others when conflict emerges, seeking understanding by listening. Often this boss works things out without anger. The boss is promoted, and the young executive tries to emulate this boss's behavior because he, too, wants to get promoted.

Our model proposes that the greater the motivation for revenge, the more likely victims will choose revenge as a coping response instead of choosing forgiveness or reconciliation. But other factors—namely, a victim's personality traits, or situational factors such as a victim's power—may channel even a high motivation for revenge into the other coping responses.

For now, we return to the beginning of these kinds of conflicts. What kinds of triggers, exactly, set off the chain reaction of events that can lead to revenge? What actions by managers and coworkers really get under the skin of the average employee, and which triggers are worse than others? The answers are not exactly what you might expect.

3

THREE TRIGGERS OF REVENGE

Why People Try to Get Even

If you prick us, do we not bleed?
If you tickle us, do we not laugh?
If you poison us, do we not die?
And if you wrong us, shall we not revenge?
—*William Shakespeare, The Merchant of Venice*

For three years, an executive in a telecommunications company led a group that was one of the highest revenue-generators in the organization. Each year the executive asked his boss for a promotion, only to hear that he "needed more experience." But after the third year, as the executive put it, "I realized my boss didn't want to promote me because my group's performance made *him* look good. So he was blocking my advancement for his own selfish purpose." When the executive discovered that his boss was interviewing other candidates—with less experience—for the position *he* wanted, he commiserated with a coworker. That's when he found out his boss had been bad-mouthing him at the company for a long time, saying that he had an "attitude problem" and couldn't be promoted. "That was it," the executive told us. "I said screw 'em. I left for another company and got the promotion I wanted and deserved."

What triggered this executive to say, essentially, "Take this job and shove it"? While most executives and managers believe that revenge is random or arbitrary action, we have discovered that it's not random; in fact, it's quite predictable. What is important for executives and managers—for all employees,

41

in fact—to understand is that revenge is a response to feeling harmed or wronged by someone else. So it's best to begin by understanding what triggers an act of revenge in the first place.

In the opening story, all three of the major triggers of revenge are in play: *goal obstruction* (the executive was being blocked from achieving his goal of a promotion); *breaking the rules and social norms* (the executive's boss violated significant social norms when he "used" the employee and then lied about it); and *damage to a reputation* (the boss told others in the company that the executive was not a cooperative player).

Goal Obstruction

Perhaps the most basic or primal motivation for revenge is when one person frustrates another in attaining some goal or reward. Psychologists call it the "frustration-aggression" response: when one is frustrated by interference in goal-directed activity, one is more likely to aggress.[1] So we aggress against the person who frustrates us—and sometimes immediately and reflexively, without much contemplation.[2] For instance, we yell and honk at the slow car in front of us that is making us late.

Similarly, parents reflexively yell at their kids when the kids, after being told five times, still have not cleaned up their rooms. And that yelling is not simply a matter of using punishment in a calculated way to get kids to cooperate and grow up to be tidier people. Often, the yelling is just emotional venting of frustration by the parent. That is, the yelling is for the parent, not the child.

But children can also vent frustration with their parents to get even. For example, Bob and his two-year-old daughter once went to the airport to greet his wife after a business trip, an absence that had made the daughter frustrated and angry. Their daughter decided to get even with her mother for being away for so long. What did she do? As Bob's wife entered the gate area, their daughter turned her back on her and gave her the "silent treatment" for ten (very long) seconds!—but then turned around and ran to Mom and gave her a big hug and kiss. Even kids know how to get even at a very early age.

By the way, frustration-aggression is often a response to inanimate objects as well. Have you ever yelled at your computer? Slapped it? Contemplated revenge against it, involving a high rooftop and a hard street below? Seems silly—after all, how can an unthinking object be taught a lesson?—and yet, most of us have done exactly this.

Consider the following example from the corporate world. As part of a broader study of conflict management, Calvin Morrill describes in *The Executive Way* how senior managers pursue their grievances against each other.[3] Morrill tells the story of two media and entertainment executives whom he nicknames the Princess of Power (head of marketing) and the Iron Man (from operations). The Princess of Power proposes a new marketing plan that would extend the production time line from six to nine months. The Iron Man views this plan as an obstruction to his goal of high-quality products, which prompts complaints from him in meetings involving the Princess of Power. Growing tired of the Iron Man's "roadblocks," the Princess of Power challenges him openly. The Iron Man responds with a couple of "grenades" to get even, which then prompts a "declaration of war" by the Princess of Power. Goal obstruction, then, led these two executives to engage in revenge to get even.

Another place where we commonly find goal obstruction as a trigger for revenge is in the halls of government. Consider the story told to us by a U.S. federal agency executive we'll call John about how he became the target of revenge. John was part of a cross-departmental task force that traveled across the United States with a high-ranking U.S. government figure, speaking to community and youth groups on "public health" policy issues. After each of the trips, each presenter from the task force was graded on performance. John was always the highest-rated presenter, which led the government official to have high regard for John, thus requesting his presence at all speaking engagements. The lowest-rated executive, from another part of the U.S. government, was angry—and envious—of John's performance. John's ratings were stopping this executive from advancing higher in the governmental power chain.

Unfortunately for John, this executive was also in charge of scheduling the presenters for each trip. When the itinerary for an upcoming trip was announced, John discovered that he was not on the list of presenters. When John's staff inquired as to why, the jealous executive offered some excuse about how busy he knew John was and that he was just trying to help John out. A little deeper digging by John's staff uncovered the obvious: John was not invited to present because the other executive wanted him out of the way so that he would not be upstaged by John again.

Outraged, John decided to get even. He asked one of his staff to raise the issue of his exclusion with the government official who was the focus of the trip. The government official was surprised by John's absence and quickly reinstated him to the speaker panel, where John then made sure he really upstaged the executive who had excluded him rather than simply outshining him as usual.

A final point we want to make about goal obstruction is how the littlest things, it seems, can trigger revenge—like who gets the best parking space. Take the case of a large bank that was forced to reduce the number of parking spaces at its downtown corporate headquarters. Specifically, the bank lost eighteen of its forty spaces, which, not surprisingly, resulted in an intense competition for the remaining twenty-two spaces. The bank CFO in charge of allocating the scarce parking spots tried to be as accommodating as he could, given the egos of the executives involved. In particular, the CIO wanted a downtown parking spot even though he did not work downtown. The CIO argued that he needed a permanent parking spot for information security purposes, which required full access to the building at all times. What made matters more complicated was that the CIO wanted the spot that the CFO had designated to the deputy director of finance, who reported directly to the CFO.

After many heated debates and intense lobbying by the CIO, the bank president decided to give the spot to the "Y2K Project Office" rather than specifically to the CIO. But everyone knew that the CIO was going to use the spot himself. The CFO was outraged and could only seethe over the CIO's successful political machinations.

But a subsequent event provided the CFO an opportunity for revenge. A few months later, some other tenants in the parking lot complained that fragments had fallen from the ceiling and damaged their cars. An analysis by the engineers recommended that the building's general contractor reinforce the wall and floor with steel beams or girders at two *discretionary* places in the garage where the bank had parking spaces. So, where to put the beams? The property management and general contractors kicked the decision up to the bank CFO. Perhaps it won't surprise you to learn that the CFO had the concrete support wall constructed right in the middle of the CIO's parking spot.

Revenge over parking spots is not limited to the executive suite. An office manager at a global manufacturing company had a free reserved parking spot in the garage, complete with a sign that said RESERVED in capital letters. One morning another executive, who was running late for a meeting, parked in the reserved spot. When the office manager arrived and found her spot occupied, she was livid. After parking in an unreserved spot next to her spot, she rushed to her office and immediately called a tow truck to remove the executive's car. She felt vindicated, but the executive was angry because he paid a towing fee and had to miss an important lunch with out-of-town executives in order to retrieve his car.

Two months later, the executive found a way to get even when he overheard the office manager talking about her grandchild's recital that afternoon and that she was looking forward to the performance. The executive went to the garage and let the air out of the office manager's tires. He then called the tow company to remove the car. Needless to say, the office manager missed her grandchild's recital. (See the following box for another example of just how petty the issues—and revenge tactics—can become when it comes to goal obstruction.)

You're Sitting in My Chair

A financial services manager tells the story of coming out of a meeting and hearing arguing in the secretarial pool. "All of the partners rushed to the scene," she said. "Once we separated the secretaries who were moving chairs and yelling at each other, we asked what was going on. What we found out stunned us. One of the secretaries had switched her chair with another secretary's. When that secretary found out, they confronted each other. So the secretary took her chair back. The other secretary stopped her and took it away from her. That led the other secretaries to 'take sides' in the dispute, and only escalated the anger and yelling. All this over a chair."

But consider yet another chair story, this one from a production floor. A quality control official of a major manufacturing plant recounted this incident: "As I was walking the plant floor, monitoring the performance of the crew, I found two individuals yelling at each other, almost to the point of fisticuffs. I intervened, separating them and asking what was going on." The answer? "He was sitting in my chair." It turns out that the production worker wanted to get even with the other production worker because he had entered his "territory" (his chair)—and getting even involved a public confrontation that might have led to a fight if the quality control official had not intervened.

While all these examples are different, they share a common theme. That is, when someone stops others from getting what they want, people get angry and want to get even. It's as simple as that, much like the sibling rivalry that many of us grew up with. Just being a roadblock to others can motivate revenge, but often a simple sense of injustice or being unfairly treated can be the motivating force.

Breaking the Rules and Social Norms

In our research in the workplace, we have been struck by just how sensitive people can be when those around them break the rules or violate social norms. Let's begin with a look at why people seek revenge when they perceive rules have been broken.

Breaking the Rules

Every organization has rules that govern how decisions are made. Whether they involve hiring and promotion or salary increases and budget allocations, those decision-making processes are subject to rules. When the rules are broken, people get angry. It's really not much different from the disputes we all had in childhood—when someone broke the rules of Capture the Flag or Monopoly, we got mad and then got even by quitting the game (or worse!). Three kinds of rule-breaking acts often cause people to exact revenge.

First, a *violation of the formal rules* is apt to trigger revenge. Consider this story of a consumer-product company manager. When his company's budget committee allocated a research grant to another group—one that didn't meet the official criteria for eligibility for such resources—the angry manager said: "The rules mean nothing anymore. With this flagrant violation, I no longer trust anybody making decisions." He then embarked on a strategy to make the other group look bad in meetings where their project was discussed.

Rule violations also occur when someone is promoted to a higher position of authority and status—but doesn't meet the promotion criteria. For example, when a young professor at a major university came up for tenure, he had failed to publish enough articles in top academic journals to warrant tenure, according to university rules. But this professor had allies who persuaded others that the rules were just guidelines and that he had such great potential that his case warranted tenure. Their argument carried the day. What made many faculty members angry was that another professor had been denied tenure even though his publication record exceeded the tenure rules. As one faculty member said: "Academia is just like *Animal Farm* . . . all pigs are equal except for some that are more equal." (For another example of rule violation, see the following box.)

Road Rage

Sometimes rules violations can lead to job-safety concerns, which also can trigger revenge. For example, when people drive too fast or recklessly on a road where a construction crew is working—endangering workers' lives—construction flaggers have been known to get even by smacking those cars with their flags—which, by the way, are made out of metal, not cloth. We heard the story of one construction crew in Seattle, for example, that was working on a bridge and had to close a lane, thereby constricting rush-hour traffic. One driver, perhaps frustrated at having his commute-time goal obstructed, decided to get even by veering right off the lane toward the flagger in an attempt to back the flagger against a barricade. The flagger, now out for revenge himself, held out his metal flag sideways as the car passed, leaving a long silver scratch across the driver's shiny sports car. Enraged, the burly driver and his burly passenger got out of the car, clearly intending to punch out the flagger. Before they could reach him, however, eight burlier construction workers dropped their jackhammers, literally picked up the driver and passenger, and stuffed them back in their car.

Changing the rules after the fact is a second common form of rule-breaking. For example, Steve joined a prestigious law firm in Los Angeles as a full partner who was to act as a *rainmaker*—that is, someone who uses his contacts to find new clients. His fourth year at the firm, Steve had an incredibly good year bringing in clients. According to the rules on dividing up end-of-year bonuses among partners, Steve had earned among the largest bonus of any partner. But other, more senior "named" partners who, according to the rules, would earn smaller bonuses than Steve that year, thought it was wrong that a new and "un-named" partner should earn more than they would. Clearly, they thought, something was wrong with their bonus-distribution formula. So, they fixed the formula so that Steve's bonus was smaller than their bonuses. Appalled, Steve first attempted to negotiate his proper bonus, but after the negotiation failed, he got even by leaving the firm and taking his contacts with him.

Third, a *breach of a formal contract* is viewed as the most objective kind of rule violation, because the rules and expectations were in writing. As an example of this type of violation, someone negotiated a formal contract with his investment bank employer, detailing promotion and salary increase schedules, but neither salary nor promotion schedules were met. The bank "just decided not to honor the contract." As the affected banker put it: "You can't even trust the paper the contract is written on."

This breach of formal contract underlies the anger of union and retired employees who find their allegedly "lifetime" benefits eliminated in corporate bankruptcy proceedings or after a corporate takeover. What many union retirees learned over the past decade was when they were promised "lifetime medical benefits" it was interpreted by the companies to be for the lifetime *of the contract* and could be revoked at the discretion of the company. For example, in the steel industry, 250,000 retirees and their spouses lost their benefits during Chapter 11 bankruptcies in the years 2000 to 2003.[4]

But unions have not stood by idly: they are trying to stop what they believe to be a breach of their collectively bargained agreements with companies. In the case of 2,900 retired union autoworkers for ArvinMeritor, a Michigan parts supplier, the union filed a lawsuit challenging ArvinMeritor's unilateral cancellation of the union members' lifetime retiree health benefits.[5] These benefits had been negotiated in 1962. A federal judge temporarily restored the benefits. Regardless of the ultimate outcome, retired union members and their spouses are using litigation to fight their battles, not just to get their money but also to get even with companies that they believe have broken a formal agreement.

Breaking the Social Norms

Not all the rules are written down, of course, or even declared as rules. Often, people come to understand that there are just some ways people do and should behave. For instance, many teams never explicitly define a rule that each member contributes equally, but usually that's the expectation. Sociologists refer to such commonly understood expectations as *social norms*. Acting in accordance with the prevailing social norms is important to people, and a violation can trigger revenge. More specifically, when someone violates the standard of honor, people distrust the violator.[6] In our studies, we have found five such social norm violations. A sixth violation—abuse of authority—applies mainly to leaders, and we cover that later in the chapter (see p. 55), in the box titled "The Bad Boss."

1. First, *shirking of job responsibilities* is viewed as a norm violation. This is a common trigger of revenge in teams, particularly when one team member does not fulfill the job responsibilities, thus leaving the other team members to carry the load. Such shirking violates an implicit, if not explicit, trust among team members to "work together," as one person described, and "share the load" equally.

Take for example two consultants, Brad and Larry. Brad was a team leader while Larry was an expert brought to the team from elsewhere in the firm. About two weeks into the project, Larry seemed to lose interest. He began to goof off at work, trying to engage other team members in wide-ranging but not project-relevant conversations. Larry would also leave the team to have long phone conversations with friends and colleagues, which was distracting and frustrating to other team members.

Brad approached Larry to address his slacking off and its impact on the team. After the meeting, Larry only became worse, even to the point of roping in one of the junior consultants to slack off as well. To make matters even worse, at the next client-status meeting, in which Larry's participation was critical, Larry called in sick. Brad and the team had to scramble to put Larry's material together as a placeholder strategy, but the client clearly saw the deficiencies in the presentation. Brad was furious with Larry—and decided to get even. When he learned that Larry had 360-degree feedback coming up, Brad met with the principal in the firm who was gathering information for Larry's review and offered a few names to be added, which the principal took. Brad then called all the people that he had added to Larry's list and gave them an earful of Larry's antics and slacking off. As a result, each of those people graded Larry very poorly. After the review, more investigation was done into Larry's performance on other teams and a clear picture emerged—and six months later, Larry was asked to leave the firm. (For another example of such norm violations, see the following box.)

Where's Bob?

Bob was a team supervisor who worked at a production plant of a telecommunications company. But Bob liked to disappear from the job to make phone calls, go to the cafeteria, or visit with other coworkers. What made matters worse, Bob expected his team members to cover for him when the senior supervisor would stop by.

The team members felt Bob wasn't carrying his fair share of the workload, and they decided to get even with a practical joke. One Friday afternoon when Bob had once again left the team to do his work for him, they took Bob's toolbox (something that Bob regarded as sacred property, to be touched only by himself) and made some improvements. The box was locked, so they removed the hinges and put a ripe banana at the bottom of the box. They then put magnetic covers over all of Bob's tools, making them nearly impossible to remove. They then rehinged the box so that Bob couldn't tell that anyone had touched it. After the weekend, Bob opened his toolbox, reeled back from the reek of rotten fruit, and screamed, "Who messed with my toolbox?!" The team kept their laughter to themselves.

2. *Broken promises* represent a second norm violation, and an action that can motivate revenge. For example, a coworker promises to help you out at a difficult client meeting, but then backs out at the last minute with no explanation. Or consider the boss who made explicit promises to support a subordinate's candidacy for a promotion, but in the end did not follow through. The subordinate's response? "My boss's word means nothing, absolutely," he told us. "I'll never trust him again."

3. *Lying* is a third social norms violation that creates feelings of distrust and outrage—for example, the boss who promises an employee a raise when, in fact, no raise was even considered. Or take the case of a coworker who claimed to have completed a contribution to a team project when it was not actually finished; as a result, the team failed to complete the project on time and incurred the wrath and anger of top management.

At one university we heard of, the duplicitous player was the president himself. Despite explicit assurances by the Office of the University President that a proposed faculty reorganization plan would never occur, the reorganization plan was announced. Subsequent protests by angry faculty and students led to university investigations into the legitimacy and the fairness of the administrative process that created the reorganization.

In the face of being lied to, then, the typical reaction by people is that they have been duped and manipulated—reactions also similar to those who were victims of broken promises—and are unable to trust the liar again.

4. *Stealing ideas or credit from others* is a fourth trigger of revenge. Whether it be a boss who replaces a subordinate's name on a report and claims public credit for it, or a team member who claims primary responsibility for an innovation despite having contributed very little, stealing credit creates a visceral response among victims—and observers.

Take the case of Roger and Annie, who worked at a well-known magazine. Roger was a very popular writer whose articles and columns created a lot of buzz among the readership. In the eyes of many who worked at the magazine, Roger was taking his fame quite seriously, acting more like a prima donna each day. In particular, his behavior frustrated Annie, Roger's copy editor.

Annie knew Roger much better than the readers did. Many of the columns that Roger submitted were riddled with factual inaccuracies, which really irritated Annie because Roger presented himself as an expert. Each month her hard work cleaning up Roger's writing, for which he and not she, got the credit, went unrecognized. When Annie tried to make a move to work with a different writer, Roger blocked her. So Annie decided to get even.

She saw her chance when the magazine was putting together a special issue, one with a large annual supplement. Given that there were more articles to edit than normal, Annie suggested that the managing editor send out unedited articles to the editorial review board while she completed the copy editing on the first batch of articles. She argued that this would speed up production and save money for the magazine. The managing editor agreed, and Annie sent out Roger's unedited articles for review.

The editorial board was aghast at the sloppiness of Roger's work. And the board members realized that if one of Roger's articles, filled with factual inaccuracies, ever slipped through the editing process and went to press, the magazine's reputation would seriously suffer. In the end, the managing editor restructured Roger's relationship with the magazine: his work now had to undergo a more complex editing process, and the magazine would downplay Roger in its advertising campaigns. Ultimately, Roger left the magazine while Annie strengthened her reputation as a talented and efficient copy editor.

5. Finally, the *disclosure of private confidences and secrets* is an action that violates a fundamental trust between people and often triggers a vengeful response. Whether it be disclosing a private matter that was supposed to be held in confidence or taking secret information and using it to personal advantage, such an action is viewed as a fundamental betrayal, a knife in the back, resulting in what one person described as "not just a splintering but a shattering of trust."

Consider the case of the CEO of a manufacturing company who had just led the firm through a series of layoffs, budget cutbacks, and salary freezes while still meeting the financial targets set by the board of directors. The CEO received a large performance bonus, which was awarded secretly—given the awkwardness of asking the employees to sacrifice while he would not have to. With a little guilt motivating him, the CEO asked the board to award bonuses to a select number of his top officers who had been instrumental in managing the company through the difficult times. The board agreed to the CEO's request.

The CEO asked the vice president of human resources to process the bonus checks personally and secretly. Normally, the vice president would do so without hesitation, but because he had been left off the list (unfairly, he felt, given his role in dealing with the human pain of the layoffs and cutbacks!), he was angry and decided to get even. The following day, news of the bonuses for executives was general knowledge, and a discussion point at every water cooler in the company. Not surprisingly, all employees were disgruntled, and sent scathing e-mail to their supervisors and managers.

Word of the anger and deep discontent made its way quickly to the CEO. The CEO investigated what had happened, and discovered the vice president of human resources had *intentionally* leaked the information. Specifically, on top of the copying machine used by many employees, he left copies of the list of executives who had received bonuses *and* the amount of bonus each executive had received. The CEO was outraged by the "violation of confidentiality" and summarily fired the vice president.

The Bad Boss

The *abuse of authority* represents a special kind of breaking social norms or codes of conduct—those to which we hold our leaders accountable. The "intolerable boss" and the "corrupt boss" represent two such types of leaders. Such bosses have become the subject of recent popular books such as *The No Asshole Rule* by Robert Sutton and *Brutal Bosses and Their Prey* by Harvey Hornstein.[7]

The *intolerable boss* is a classic example of abuse in action. Specifically, such bosses are hypercritical, overdemanding, overly harsh, and even cruel in their dealings with subordinates across time. There was, for example, the story of the financial services executive who worked his subordinates sixteen to eighteen hours a day, seven days a week. In addition, the boss would send his subordinates e-mail messages at home and would call them on the phone at home *at all hours*. As one employee described it: "I felt exploited and abused and the victim of 'management by psychosis.'" Another subordinate said: "He is a micromanager and he sucks the joy out of my life." When these subordinates began sending anonymous notes to human resources describing the boss's abuse, attempting to get him fired, HR investigated his behavior and then sent a formal report to senior management. While the boss did not lose his job, he was nevertheless infuriated that his behavior had been reported to senior management. The boss modified his behavior to some degree, but left the company three months later to join another financial services company.

The *corrupt boss* is another classic example of abuse in action. Such bosses were cited as those who padded expense reports or made sure they "flew in first class *at company expense*, while the rest of the team flew in coach class on the airplane." These were bosses who would hire their kids for a prime job, or overlook theft of company resources by their friends. As one person described her boss: "He thought he should be treated as lord and king, and above the law. He called us his 'subjects,' who were lucky to have a job. Little did he realize that his subjects were plotting a revolt."

Damaging a Reputation

Reputation damage occurs when people believe they are the targets of interpersonal attacks that have the effect of impugning or undermining their social identity. Such attacks include *public criticism, wrong or unfair accusations, and insults to one's self or social group*. Each of these attacks is viewed as violating an implicit trust that one's dignity and respect should be inviolate, often triggering the most intense desire for revenge.

Public criticism is viewed as a direct and focused attack on one's social reputation. Such criticism is not only negative but usually personal and demeaning. For example, one boss brought the whole department together and singled out one employee for poor performance in harsh and angry terms, even making fun of the employee's lack of skills and abilities. According to the employee, he felt he had "lost face," and felt "belittled and degraded" and "emotionally scarred" as a result of this attack. Note how the language reflects the expression of feeling an altered social identity. Such public criticism can motivate revenge, even when the criticism is fair and true. Employees often believe that harsh criticism, if it needs to occur at all, should occur behind a manager's closed door, not out in the open office or on the shop floor. To deliver such criticism publicly is perceived as a gratuitous attack on the recipient's reputation, an attack that motivates revenge.

Consider the case of a telecommunications company division president who was having difficulty managing the department's operations and employees. Morale and productivity began to plummet. As news of the department's struggles spread throughout the company, the CEO demanded changes. In a desperate attempt to improve employee productivity, the division president decided to use fear as a motivator. He brought three scapegoats whom he had identified as the "problem children" to a public forum and scolded them in front of hundreds for their bad attitudes and poor performance. Given no chance to defend themselves or refute the charges against them, the three employees decided to get even for their public humiliation and the emotional stress it caused them. They submitted a formal complaint to human resources describing how they had been unfairly treated, and they solicited similar stories of mistreatment from other employees who had worked with the division president. In the end, the three employees gathered hundreds of such stories, which they forwarded to the vice president of human resources. This led to a company investigation of the division president and ultimately to his termination.

Being *accused wrongly or unfairly* represents a second type of attack on one's reputation. A wrongful accusation involves a person being blamed for a mistake or failure, when that person was not in fact at fault. For example, a consumer products manager recounted how she was accused by her boss, a senior marketing manager, of stealing ideas—when in fact it was the boss who had stolen the ideas from her!

An unfair accusation is similar to a wrongful accusation in that both are untrue. But for the managers and working professionals in our studies, an unfair accusation typically reflected a "gross misrepresentation of the facts" about something that had happened, while a wrongful accusation was a simple assertion that someone had done something they actually hadn't done. An example of an unfair accusation involves a telecommunications executive who blamed her team for failure, even though the team had done its best and in spite of some questionable decisions by the boss. Her accusation left team members feeling discredited and that these accusations "did not do justice" to them.

Feeling unfairly or wrongly accused can also lead one to get even through legal action. Consider the case of Rick Neuheisel, now the UCLA head football coach, but formerly head coach of the University of Washington Huskies. Neuheisel was quite a successful football coach for the University of Washington. Over four seasons as head coach, Neuheisel had a 33–16 record, including a Rose Bowl victory in 2001 and a No. 3 national ranking.

But in 2003, Neuheisel was fired by the University of Washington athletic director because of his participation in high-stakes NCAA tournament basketball pools the previous two years. Neuheisel admitted he was part of a four-man team that won $20,000 in 2002 and won the same pool in 2003—but he also claimed that he did not believe participation in the pools was a violation of NCAA rules. Although the NCAA explicitly prohibits gambling on college athletics by its players, coaches, and other personnel, Neuheisel produced an e-mail written by the University of Washington athletic director that said wagering in off-campus NCAA tournament pools was *not* a violation.

Neuheisel therefore felt wrongfully accused by the University of Washington and unfairly terminated as head football coach—and he filed a wrongful-termination lawsuit against the university. After twenty-one months, the university settled with Neuheisel in the amount of $4.5 million, and Neuheisel felt vindicated not just by the settlement amount but also in the restoration of his reputation after the accusations. But the story was not over. In 2007, when Neuheisel was named head football coach at his alma mater, UCLA, he recruited a highly rated quarterback *away from* the University of Washington![8]

Finally, an *insult to one's self or social group* represents a third kind of attack on social identity that we have observed. We found that insults on a personal level typically involved name-calling, as in questioning the person's intellectual capacities by referring to the employee as a moron, or in challenging a male employee's lack of assertiveness by stating, "He was a wimp; probably had no balls." Insults to social group involve any attack not on a specific individual but on a group to which the individual belongs by gender, ethnicity, age, religion, or other characteristics, and also attacks on the individual's professional background, such as which school was attended or what was studied.

An example of the latter that led to mild revenge is an engineering firm employee who was working on his MBA. He was disrespected by his coworkers as lacking intelligence, in part because he had what they called an "inferior" college degree (that is, they judged that his business degree was less rigorous than their engineering degrees). After losing an informal debate at work about politics one time too many, where he was once again disrespected, he went out of his way to bring in newspaper articles to work that proved he was right. He not only felt vindicated, he enjoyed rubbing their faces in it.

For a more disturbing example of an insult to one's social group, consider the story of Angie, an African American middle manager at a manufacturing company. Angie had worked her way up the managerial ranks to become head of customer service, and along the way, earned an MBA through an evening program at a local university.

Unfortunately, her boss, the vice president of marketing, was a known bigot who resented the fact that Angie had been promoted over his protests. He did not feel that the position should be filled by a woman, let alone by an African American. So, in public meetings, he would ask her to go get the coffee and would ignore her comments in the meeting. When she was out of the room, he would refer to her in the most egregious racist and sexist terms. Some of the other managers laughed along with the boss, but some remained quiet and later told Angie about these attacks.

Feeling angry and powerless, Angie raised the issue with the HR department, who then investigated. The boss's response was to blame Angie, saying that she was just making things up and clearly could not handle the pressures of the job. Just as Rick Neuheisel did, Angie felt her identity had been damaged and decided to seek legal recourse. She filed a lawsuit against her boss and her company for sexual harassment, focusing on the hostile work environment created by the boss because of his offensive language and demeaning behavior toward her. The outcome of the lawsuit is still pending.

The Injustice of It All

Of the three major revenge-triggering offenses explored in this chapter—goal obstruction, breaking the rules and social norms, and damage to reputations—what is it about breaking rules and norms and about damaging reputations, in particular, that motivates revenge? It's the injustice of it. That is, victims of such triggers judge these actions as injustices committed against them.[9] This is why revenge can seem like the right response: revenge is the attempt to restore justice by evening the score, and the perception of these three kinds of injustice, each alone and especially in combination, will tend to lead to revenge.[10]

For decades now, scholars of workplace psychology have tested and documented the various ways that employees perceive elements of their environs as fair and unfair.[11] Much of this research started by studying how people in general perceive certain outcomes, actions, and policies (for instance, in the legal environment). Interestingly, they found that the principles of justice by which citizens judge legal authorities and their actions (for example, police making arrests, judges enforcing courtroom procedures, and juries weighing monetary damages) are nearly the same principles by which employees judge organizational authorities (bosses conducting performance appraisals, managers implementing layoff procedures, and committees awarding bonuses). Essentially, in both contexts, three basic principles of justice apply: procedural justice, interactional justice, and distributive justice. Interestingly, these three principles also correspond to two of the three triggers of revenge we have found in our own research.

First, *procedural justice* is about the perceived fairness of the decision-making process by which an outcome is determined. Such processes are perceived as more fair if they have certain features.[12] For instance, were the rules applied consistently, or were some people above the law? Was accurate information used, or was the decision based on poorly researched "facts" and gossip? Did the decision makers have any conflicts of interest, perhaps by somehow benefiting from one particular outcome over another? Did those who received the outcomes have any say or input into the decision, or was the decision merely imposed on them without consultation? Can the decision be appealed? Overall, was it ethical? These questions represent the principles and features of procedural justice that people, whether they be defendants or employees, care about and expect to see.

The breaking of rules and social norms is a procedural injustice. When bosses and coworkers don't follow the rules and make bad decisions, employees perceive that something is wrong and unfair, if not corrupt, about the process. Worse, perhaps, is that if the process is not fixed somehow—such as enforcing the rules through revenge—then more bad decisions will occur. In fact, if nobody follows the rules, then civic order breaks down and the employees are left with chaos. In our tenure example earlier in the chapter, this is what so disturbed the faculty who watched the rules be ignored to one candidate's benefit and another's detriment. Or consider the executive who said, "The rules mean nothing anymore. With this flagrant violation, I no longer trust anybody making decisions."

Second, *interactional justice* is about the quality of the interactions that the decision makers have with those who receive the outcomes of those decisions.[13] For instance, how did the police officer treat the arrested person? With respect and dignity? Or, how did the boss deliver the news about impending layoffs? Were the affected employees given the information ahead of time? Did the boss tell the truth about how people were picked to be laid off? Did the company treat them with respect, or have security escort them out the door right after being informed of the layoff?

A damaged reputation comes from interactional injustice. When bosses belittle or demean employees after a decision, employees often feel diminished, and unfairly so. Thus, the employees may attempt to punish the boss and regain their reputations through revenge. This is why firms get into trouble when they add insult to injury by having security escort freshly dismissed employees off the premises so that they cannot steal any office supplies or sabotage anything. In essence, such employees are treated like would-be criminals. Companies do this precisely because they are worried about revenge. Ironically, such insensitive and insulting actions just increase dismissed employees' motivation for revenge. Sure, the company prevents the dismissed employee from stealing some supplies or erasing a hard drive, but whatever can be done to get even from the outside, the ex-employee is now far more motivated to do—such as sue the company for wrongful termination. It also tends to reduce the respect surviving employees feel for the company, increasing the chance of revenge by people who were not laid off.

Finally, *distributive justice* is about the perceived fairness of how outcomes are distributed among different people. Do people get the size of outcomes they deserve? For instance, does the punishment fit the crime? That is, is a prison sentence proportional to the magnitude of the crime committed? For a workplace example, is an employee's pay proportional to the efforts and contribution that employee makes? The perception of such outcome fairness depends, in part, upon what somebody else is getting. Does my partner in crime receive an equally stiff sentence? Does my coworker get paid the same for the same job description, and if not, is that pay discrepancy fair? The perception of outcome fairness is also influenced, in part, by merely whether the outcome is favorable. That is, did I get what I wanted or expected?

Distributive justice seems like it might fit the trigger of goal obstruction, but it does not necessarily do so. That is, goal obstruction is *sometimes* about distributive injustice, but often it is too knee-jerk to be about anything. Sometimes people are merely frustrated, and then quickly vent that frustration before they can evaluate the fairness or unfairness of the trigger. In one study, experienced workers and managers rated the three triggers. The result? They viewed breaking rules and social norms and damaging reputations as completely unjust—but they did *not* view goal obstruction as unjust. This is one reason why we say that revenge is often *but not always* about justice.

Through the stories in this chapter of real people and the variety of triggers they experienced in the workplace, it begins to become clear how things, big and small, can create the desire for revenge. Most triggers are perceived as injustices—injustices that may need to be corrected through revenge. Whether the trigger actually leads someone further down the path to actually taking revenge depends on their analysis of *why* the person harmed or wronged them and finding someone to be at fault. For revenge to follow, someone must be to blame. But whom to blame and how much to blame? Let the blame game begin!

4

YOU STARTED IT!

The Mind Game Inside the Blame Game

It's not whether you win or lose,
it's how you place the blame.

—*Oscar Wilde*

Consider the following story of a university department head, Jim, who handled complaints about professors from students. One day, a student, Sherry, lodged a complaint against a professor, Ted. Sherry complained that Professor Ted had harmed her by giving her a low grade that she did not deserve. When Jim asked her to talk to Professor Ted about the grade, she said there would be no point, because Ted was biased against her. Actually, she claimed that he even *hated* her and openly discriminated against her in class by not calling on her and by demeaning what comments she did make. In Sherry's mind, her motive for lodging an official complaint wasn't so much the poor grade as her perception that Ted treated her badly.

To Jim, this didn't sound like something that Ted would do, but it was Jim's job to keep an open mind and look into the complaint. When he talked to Ted, Ted claimed that the grade was fair, that he did not discriminate against Sherry, and he wasn't even aware that she felt this way. In fact, he really didn't pay much attention to her at all.

When Jim spoke again to Sherry and told her that Ted felt no animosity toward her, Sherry was unconvinced. She claimed other students agreed with her that Ted discriminated against her and hated her. Jim told Sherry that claming Ted hated her was a serious matter, and she needed to provide more than just an assertion. How did she know for sure that he hated her? Did Ted ever say that, or insult her in class? No. Did he ever refuse to meet with her? No. She said, "I can just tell." When Jim demanded better evidence, then Sherry decided that he was out to get her too. Feeling even more outraged than before, Sherry insulted Jim and left the meeting. In her mind, she had interpreted ambiguous events to mean that others were conspiring to do her harm. Sherry dropped the official complaint, but she then proceeded to bad-mouth both Ted and Jim to other students.

Here's the funny thing. Ted never really did have it in for Sherry; he had paid no special attention to her; he never thought about her outside of class. Not at first, that is. But after all Sherry's complaining and bad-mouthing, you can bet that Ted knew who Sherry was; he came to hate her for real, and eventually he *was* out to get her. From Ted's point of view, he was the victim of an unfounded complaint by an irresponsible student. He was up for tenure, and he worried that Sherry's complaints had hurt his reputation at a most critical time in his career. Good thing that Sherry never had to take another class from Ted, or their feud would have escalated. All Ted could do was bad-mouth her to other faculty, which he did.

Why do such disagreements get out of hand? Why did Sherry become so convinced that Ted was out to get her, especially when Ted barely knew who she was? How could Sherry be so wrong? That is, what kinds of mental tricks and mind games was she playing on herself, and how did those tricks lead her to blame Ted so harshly, thereby justifying her attempts to destroy Ted's reputation? How could she be so sure that she was the victim and Ted was the villain, while Ted was so sure that she was the villain while he was the victim? And how innocent was Ted, really?

Alternate Realities

The key to understanding and predicting revenge lies in how people make sense of the bad things that happen to them. Sometimes this sense-making process meets the standards of the scientific method—that is, people gather all the facts in a dispassionate manner in pursuit of the truth about the bad thing that happened, which results in a rational and accurate judgment and assignment of blame.

Unfortunately, that approach to sense making is not how we as human beings typically proceed in pursuit of the truth.[1] Much research has shown that people are less scientific and more sloppy and self-serving in how they make sense of bad things that happen to them. The story of Jim, Sherry, and Ted is a classic example.

Examining such disputes reveals a lot about the blaming process—a lot of *ugliness* about the blaming process, to be precise. Consider, for example, your favorite couple who broke up, then each came to you with their side of the story of what really happened. Or think of two coworkers who came to hate each other, but both still liked you and talked to you. Maybe you've even mediated conflicts. In the mediation process, most likely, you got to hear each side of this he-said-she-said conflict, whether you wanted to hear it or not. (Usually not.) Listening to the competing accounts of the *same* events, you may have wondered if the people talking to you had really participated in the same conflict, or if one or both of them were pathological liars. Why? Because instead of hearing one story with one protagonist and one antagonist, you heard two stories with two protagonists and two antagonists. To hear him tell it, he was caring, virtuous, and reasonable, while she was selfish, immoral, and cynical. To hear her tell it, she was altruistic, principled, and realistic, while he was nosy, defensive, and calculating. Although their competing accounts just don't reconcile, both people very well may have told the truth about the conflict as they saw it; they just could not agree on who was to blame. Then they got even by bad-mouthing each other to you.

To illustrate how subjective and ego-defensively biased reality can become in conflict, consider a classic psychology study, "They Saw a Game."[2] In 1951, a big football game between Princeton and Dartmouth was unusually rough, with many penalties and both quarterbacks forced off the field with broken bones. The controversial game sparked furious newspaper editorials. Whose fault was it that the game got so out of hand? The Princeton community mostly blamed the Dartmouth team while the Dartmouth community mostly blamed the Princeton team. Professors Albert Hastorf of Dartmouth College and Hadely Cantril of Princeton University found this instance of "selective perception" too good not to study. So one week after the game, they invited psychology students from each campus to complete questionnaires about the event. Some students had attended the game; others only watched the game film.

When asked which team started the rough play, 86 percent of Princeton students thought Dartmouth started it, whereas only 36 percent of Dartmouth students thought Dartmouth started it. Some students were instructed to count the number of infractions they saw as they watched the game film. Princeton students counted twice as many infractions for the Dartmouth team as for the Princeton team, whereas Dartmouth students saw both teams make an equal number of infractions.

How's that? Didn't they both watch the *same* game film? Yes, they did watch the same film, but they did not *see* the same game! One explanation is that their need to defend their egos—to be associated with the side of moral virtue, making the other side the aggressive villain—filtered what they noticed in their environment. Each side noticed more facts that supported their own view than contradicted it. Hastorf and Cantril found, then, that "there is no such 'thing' as a 'game' existing 'out there' in its own right which people merely 'observe.' The 'game' 'exists' for a person and is experienced by him only in so far as certain happenings have significances in terms of his purpose."[3] More simply, this suggests a twist on the old saying, "I'll believe it when I see it." Perhaps it'd be more accurate as, "I'll see it when I believe it."

Blame, More or Less

Clearly, we are not unbiased sense makers of our environment. We selectively pay attention to and remember most that which serves our interests best. (Although not *all* biases and judgment errors are influenced by self-interest, many are.)[4] Biased sense making in turn biases how victims assign blame.[5]

Blame is everything. How a wrong or a harm can transform into the sense of injustice, which may escalate into revenge, depends on how one makes sense of the harm or wrongdoing. If one can blame another person, pain and confusion convert to anger and determination, and thus revenge becomes more likely.[6] It is the assignment of blame that is at the foundation of the rationality and morality of revenge.

In our revenge research, we find evidence of victims acting as intuitive jurists in the aftermath of harm. That is, victimized employees want to understand the offender's intentions before determining the appropriate "sentence" or response.[7] Victims desperately want to know *why* they were harmed.[8] Fundamentally, was the harm intentional or not? If intentional, was it due to opportunism or maliciousness? For example, a victim might ask, "Did X have something to gain professionally by hurting me, and thus it's not personal? Or does X simply hate me, and it is personal?" If not intentional, was it an honest accident or negligence? That is, even though X did not wish it to happen, was it unforeseeable, or was it something X could—and *should*—have foreseen and prevented?[9] It is the answers to these questions that determine how much victims blame their offenders.[10] They often obsess about this, both privately and publicly.[11]

Go back to the story that began this chapter. In her conflict with Professor Ted, Sherry wanted to understand why she received low grades and why Ted did not react in class to her comments the way she hoped. She speculated about Ted's motives openly, with fellow students and with Jim, and concluded that Ted's actions were intentional and that he hated her.

Generally, victims overattribute intent to offenders' actions. Victims see intent behind most acts of harm, even when there is no intent. That is, most acts of harm must be, the victims think, motivated by an intent to harm.[12] Thus, accidents often are not seen as accidents; and when offenders really do cause harm intentionally (as in a layoff or a denied promotion), victims tend to see a more sinister, personal motive for the harm than the relatively benign and clichéd explanation from management: "It's not personal; it's what's best for the company."

In our studies, we have found two kinds of motives featured in the more intentional attributions—selfishness and malevolence.[13] A selfish offender causes harm for personal profit, picking the victim purely based on opportunity. Sometimes, the victim is picked as a *mark*—that is, somebody who has something the offender wants or is somehow integral to the offender's goals. Here the harm is an act of commission in that the victim is consciously targeted. Other times, the victim isn't targeted at all: the victim isn't in the offender's equation and thus the harm to the victim is just an unfortunate side-effect of the offender's goal-directed behavior. For instance, the victim was in the way, and the offender chose not to stop or otherwise avoid the victim.

A *malevolent* offender causes harm for the sake of inflicting pain on the victim. Here, the victim is consciously targeted, with malice. Malevolent harm differs from selfish harm: the malevolent offender targets the victim not because the victim has something the offender wants but because the offender enjoys making *that particular* victim feel pain. That is, here it truly is personal. Malevolent harm is, by our definition, the most intentional attribution one can make about the motives of the offender.

Revisiting the conflict between Professor Ted and Sherry, we see that what motivated Sherry's complaint was her belief that Professor Ted hated her—that he treated her badly in class, ignoring her because he enjoyed humiliating her, not because, perhaps, he didn't see her half-raised hand.

"Just the Facts"

In the 1960s television show *Dragnet*, Los Angeles police detective Joe Friday and his partner Bill Gannon would appear at crime scenes to interview victims and witnesses—part of their investigation to assign blame and make an arrest. When interviewees became emotional or provided their theory about what happened, Sgt. Friday would remind them that he was asking for "just the facts." Unfortunately, when we assign blame, we act less like Joe Friday and more like the victims and witnesses that he and Gannon interviewed. We have trouble separating theory from fact, speculation from observation. (To illustrate, next time you listen to a coworker rant about what someone else did wrong, pay attention to how your coworker mixes up what the coworker knows the wrongdoer actually did with speculation about why the wrongdoer did it, presenting both as equally factual.)

In this blame game, people will search for many facts to test their theories—some facts that may discount the offender's responsibility for the action, and some facts that may exaggerate the offender's responsibility for the action.[14] For example, there may be mitigating circumstances that create a reasonable doubt in people's minds, such as an explanation that top management was pressuring the offender to behave badly. In this case, revenge against the offender is less likely. Alternatively, compounding and amplifying circumstances, such as overly supportive friends, family, and coworkers, may reinforce the victim's early, paranoid beliefs about the offender's motives as overly sinister.[15] "Yeah, you could be right; I bet the boss is out to get you!" In that case, revenge is more likely.

In Sherry's case, she searched for facts. She noted every averted glance, every failure to praise her contribution when she spoke up in class. She asked other students if they saw what she saw. We suspect that Sherry's friends, like many friends, wanted to show empathy toward her distress, and thus did not outright contradict her early suspicions of Ted's behaviors. Thus Sherry may have misinterpreted as agreement her friends' vague, comforting comments like, "Well, I suppose that's possible" or "*If* that's what happened, *then* it's certainly wrong."

And this is the problem: a mind game tends to go on inside the blame game. That is, in trying to make sense of what actually happened, victims' minds often play tricks on them,[16] sometimes aided by the misguided "help" of their friends and coworkers. As a result, victims may see things that aren't there, and maybe never were there, such as a sinister motive.[17] They find "facts" that don't exist, and they don't even know they are tricking themselves.[18] They collect evidence that is incomplete and unconfirmed, and then misinterpret it. Such mind games inside the blame game make blaming quite a biased, error-prone process. Put simply, compared to the legal system, workplace victims do sloppy detective work, apply low standards for what constitutes evidence, and then judge self-servingly.

Much research shows that such sense-making processes about conflict and blame are biased—that is, they often produce more blame than the offender deserves.[19] The exaggerated blame comes from an obsessive, self-centered, and ego-defensive process. Victims spend an inordinate amount of time piecing together what happened and what should be done. They see the conflict primarily from their own perspective, where they are the central players. Moreover, victims choose beliefs that bolster their self-esteem such that conflict is usually the *other* party's fault, not their own. The other party is the hateful aggressor, whereas oneself is the sympathetic and innocent victim.[20]

The Mind Games We Play

Drawing on our earlier work with our colleague Rod Kramer,[21] and on Rod's own work on paranoia inside organizations,[22] we now discuss a few specific individual biases and error-riddled mental processes that impact the blaming process. These biases include *hyper-vigilance, obsession, exaggerated self-reference, exaggerated perceptions of conspiracy, actor-observer bias, sinister attribution error, confirmation bias,* and *social information.* One more mental process, the *biased punctuation of conflict history,* deserves in-depth examination, and we cover that one in a separate section.

Hyper-Vigilance

Even a rarely paranoid person is often somewhat more paranoid when victimized, and particularly so when victimized inside an organization. Some scholars suggest that some level of vigilance is actually good for employees.[23] Given the often competitive and political nature of organizational life, vigilance increases the likelihood that individuals will detect threats and opportunities in time to respond effectively to them. For instance, knowing who else may be competing for a coveted promotion, an aspiring employee can package an application to highlight relative strengths over the competition and defend relative weaknesses. Also, in electoral politics, advance information of a smear campaign from a competitor could allow a candidate to mount a timely defense, rather than get surprised.

Of course, people can have too much vigilance—vigilance that creates distrust, distraction, and crippling distress. Moreover, such *hyper*-vigilant employees overprocess information, prompting the drawing of erroneous inferences.[24] The hyper-vigilant employee scrutinizes every social interaction for hidden meaning and sinister purpose, dissecting every act, no matter how seemingly benign, for hints of insult, humiliation, and derogation, and feels harmed or threatened thereby. Even the meaningless averted glance or failure to return a greeting takes on sinister significance and malevolent import, thus increasing the likelihood of revenge.

That is what happened to Sherry. At some point during the semester, perhaps after receiving her first poor grade on an assignment, Sherry began scrutinizing everything Professor Ted did. She read into how quickly he called on her in class, and when he didn't call on her. Once she showed up for his office hours (unannounced, without appointment), and he wasn't there, which she then read to mean he was avoiding students, if not avoiding her.

Obsession

Victims—at least those who consider revenge—obsess about their situation. Obviously, these are not happy thoughts; instead, negative thoughts about the offense replay repeatedly in their heads. They imagine how they might have handled it differently. For instance, if someone insults you, and you are so stunned that all you can do is mumble off a lame response, what do you do next? If you're like many people, you replay the put-down in your head, try out different responses, and a few hours later you finally think up the perfect comeback! To quote Bill Waterson in the guise of Calvin of the comic strip *Calvin & Hobbes*, "Well, remember what you said, because in a day or two, I'll have a witty and blistering retort! You'll be devastated THEN!"

Empirical studies have shown that obsession following negative events tends to increase negative thinking about those events, and also prompts a pessimistic attribution style when trying to explain why the events happened.[25] Like depressed people considering suicide, some victims fall into a hole that they have a hard time seeing out of. They see mostly the negative—what the offender did, how much it hurt, how the offender is such a jerk, and so on—and downplay the positive. Moreover, when making attributions about the offender's motives, this negative thinking makes them more pessimistic. That is, they may not give the offender the benefit of the doubt. Somewhat ironically, obsession also appears to increase individuals' confidence in their interpretations—that is, the more they think about an event, the *surer* they are of their interpretation of that event, even without any new supporting information.[26] Thus, the more victims obsess about the insults they have experienced, the more convinced they become that the insults were intentional and that they signify larger and hidden threats.

Consider the story of Amy, an office manager at a major university. "I was sure that senior leadership was out to get me," she told us. At first, she realized she was being left off of office memos that were key to her job, and soon she saw she was excluded from meetings about her own budget responsibilities. The more she thought about it, the more convinced she became that her bosses were out to get her—and as she put it, she began to connect the dots. "I was so sure that these dots existed and I could see them more clearly with each day." But she added, "Later I realized I was connecting dots that didn't exist."

Exaggerated Self-Reference

Exaggerated self-reference is a person's belief that others' actions involve the person, even though there is insufficient information to confirm, or even suggest, that the others' actions regard the person at all. By *involve* and *regard* we mean that the others' actions are caused by, or intended to impact, the person. For example, suppose an employee walks down the hall past an open office, and just as the employee passes the open door, the managers in the office close the door. The employee then reflects upon the incident, hypothesizing the possible reasons why the managers shut the door *just then:* "They were probably talking about me." To reach this conclusion, the employee has ignored or dismissed plausible alternative hypotheses, such as "They didn't want *anyone* to hear their private conversation" or that it's just plain coincidence. Basically, the employee has favored the self-referential explanation over the non-self-referential explanations, even though the latter may be more likely.

Exaggerated self-reference can lead to an overly intentional attribution where malevolent motives are assigned to benign or random events. For example, consider any accident that is mistakenly perceived as intentional. Our colleague Rod Kramer also provides the example of the employee who spends a lot of time thinking about the boss—and assumes incorrectly that the boss is spending as much time thinking about the employee.[27] Thus, when the boss's actions affect the employee, the employee is certain that the effect was intended. After all, anyone who was clearly thinking about someone else that much must have considered the effects the actions would have on that other person, and therefore the effects must be intentional. But although the actions may be intentional, often the effects are accidental, as the boss, *too busy thinking about the boss's boss*, simply neglected to consider how the employee might be affected.

We have seen exactly this kind of conflict with students. For instance, Sherry seemed to believe that Professor Ted spent as much time thinking about her as she did about him. And although she didn't explicitly say it, her complaint showed that she thought she was so important to Ted that he was spending his days thinking up ways to humiliate her.

Another student we know, however, openly displayed this type of exaggerated self-reference. This story involves Tom (and is told from Tom's viewpoint). One Sunday, Tom received a lengthy, angry e-mail from one of his students, whom he had made fun of in class when he playfully twisted an in-class comment the student had made. Usually Tom can tell, as a semester progresses, which students would like such comedic, improvisational treatment of their in-class comments and which would not, and he only picks on those students who seem confident and who like to talk and laugh a lot in class. But this time he'd gotten it wrong. Although this student did talk a lot and laughed at Tom's other jokes, he did not want his own comments to became comedy material—and he let Tom know this. So far, no problem. However, the student also wrote in the same e-mail: "Let's call off the war," adding that he believed that Tom was trying to humiliate him because Tom personally didn't like him.

In reality, Tom barely knew who this student was! Tom did not think about him outside class, and certainly did not plan humiliations for him. Yet this student was so certain he was the center of Tom's world that he composed and sent this e-mail message.

Exaggerated Perceptions of Conspiracy

Another perception that motivates revenge behavior is the *exaggerated perception of conspiracy* associated with paranoid thoughts.[28] Here, the paranoid perceiver tends to view the actions of others in the organization as more tightly connected or coordinated than they actually are. That is, the paranoid perceiver "connects the dots," even when randomly placed dots should not be connected, in much the same way ancient astrologers connected randomly strewn stars to form patterns known as constellations. For example, Anita is turned down for promotion to project leader of a cross-functional team, because, she is told, "some teammates question your ability to lead." Anita, feeling stunned and hurt, begins entertaining paranoid thoughts about how many teammates said that, and which teammates, and even whether they coordinated their negative recommendations. She might think, "It wasn't just Sally in Marketing; I bet Terry and Diego bad-mouthed me too, or at least they all probably talked about it." This may lead her to question Diego: "Did you know what Sally was going to do? Were you in on it?"

Another example of the exaggerated perceptions of conspiracy is President Lyndon Johnson, who manifested many signs of organizational paranoia as he fought his critics over management of the Vietnam War. As we describe in our work with Rod Kramer, Johnson once confided to his aide and eventual biographer, Doris Kearns-Goodwin, that he viewed the attacks against him as part of a vast concerted conspiracy to undo his presidency. "Two or three intellectuals started it all, you know. They produced all the doubt, they and the columnists in the *Washington Post*, the *New York Times*, *Newsweek*, and *Life*. And it spread and spread,"

Johnson said. "Then the communists stepped in. They control the three networks, you know, and the forty major outlets of communication. It's all in the FBI reports. They prove everything. Not just about the reporters, but about the professors too."[29]

Actor-Observer Bias

The actor-observer bias represents another bias in the causal analysis that can motivate revenge.[30] When attributing blame to a *particular* actor, how individuals attribute motives depends in part upon whether the individuals are the actors themselves judging their own actions, or mere observers judging someone else's actions. Specifically, actors who judge their own bad actions favor external or situational causes; observers who judge the actions of some other actor favor causes internal to the actor, such as personality traits. For example, an employee judging his own work performance might say, "I'm not working hard because performance isn't tied to pay, and the pay is so little anyway." A coworker observing and judging the employee's behavior might conclude, "He's not working hard because he's lazy."[31] Pay is an external attribution while laziness is an internal attribution.

In assigning blame in conflict, the actor-observer bias may play an important role. Victims are biased to judge the motivations behind the offender's harms as being internal and thus intentional. Therefore, fewer offenders will be given the benefit of the doubt, such as that they may have been forced to do what they did, or that the harm was just accidental. Moreover, when judging one's own harms toward the other, one is biased to judge one's own motivations as external, and thus not intentional, or at least not mean-spirited.

Road rage provides a common example of the actor-observer bias in conflicts. When one driver is cut off in traffic by another and has to slam on the brakes to avoid an accident, the first driver may scream at the second, "You incompetent jerk!" Incompetence and jerkishness are *internal trait* attributions. That is, the first driver, knowing *nothing* about the second except that the second driver cut off the first, is *certain* the second driver possesses these traits. The second driver, trying to determine how the first driver just got cut off, wonders aloud, "Did I just do that? I wish I'd gotten more sleep last night so that I could pay more attention like I usually do." The second driver never exclaims, "I am such a jerk!" Lack of sleep is an *external* attribution; the second driver avoids the internal attributions of aggressiveness and incompetence.

Sinister Attribution Error

Given such biases and errors, it is no surprise that people also succumb to what Rod Kramer calls the "sinister attribution error."[32] That is, when individuals overattribute sinister and malevolent motives to others' actions (for example, "That wasn't just carelessness or even just selfishness; that was pure meanness"), they may perceive harmful intent or believe they are being belittled even in otherwise seemingly benign social encounters. This error occurs even in the face of ambiguous information about another's motives, when rational people would decide they just can't know what the offender's motives were. But people aren't rational and don't decide they can't know; rather, they conclude that motives must have been hostile and sinister.[33]

A vivid example of the sinister attribution error comes from a specific event in the TV quiz show scandals of the 1950s. Richard Goodwin described the events that led Herb Stempel to take revenge against NBC executives who decided to replace him with Charles Van Doren as the star of the popular quiz show, *Twenty One*.[34] Goodwin describes the "triggering event" that pushed Stempel toward revenge. It occurred after a charity show in which Stempel and Van Doren participated in a rematch. As Stempel described it, "After the show, [Van Doren] was talking to some people behind stage, and I went over to shake his hand, and he completely ignored me. It was like I wasn't even there." Goodwin writes: "The story was an illuminating metaphor. Whatever Van Doren's flaws, he was not a snob. He was much too well bred to spurn a handshake. *He just hadn't seen Stempel, and Stempel had interpreted that momentary inattention as confirmation of his most painful misconceptions.*"[35] (Italics added here.)

In other words, Stempel had misinterpreted Van Doren's actions. He had perceived a sinister motive in Van Doren. Given his angry rumination and obsession over being unfairly removed from *Twenty-One*, and the sense of betrayal that accompanied those emotions, Stempel decided to get even with both Van Doren and the network executives by testifying before Congress as to how the results of *Twenty-One* were rigged.

Confirmation Bias

Reinforcing this sinister attribution error is the *confirmation bias*.[36] The confirmation bias is the tendency for people to seek only information that proves their initial opinions and hypotheses correct. Yet information that proves those hypotheses *incorrect* is actually more useful logically. That is, it's easier to disprove something than to prove something. For example, suppose we tell you that all members of a species of a bird, which we'll call the flip-flapper, are red. How many red flip-flappers do you need to see to prove to yourself that our hypothesis is correct? One? Two? Ten? A hundred? A thousand? The more red flip-flappers you see, the more confident you become that all flip-flappers are red. But you have to see a lot, and confidence builds slowly. But suppose you see one *green* flip-flapper? You know our hypothesis is wrong. It only took one bird sighting to disprove it. Rational decision makers should seek both kinds of information, and place more weight on information that *disproves* their theories.[37]

In workplace revenge, victims should seek information to disprove their initial, suspicious attributions. Unfortunately, victims are biased toward seeking confirmation of their worst suspicious fears, looking to prove their paranoid theories. For example, David gets fired, and he suspects it's because a customer complained about him to his boss. David then goes looking for evidence that the customer complained, including trying to contact the customer, asking coworkers about the customer, and interrogating his boss about whether the boss spoke with the customer. What David does not look for, however, is evidence that he was fired for another reason, such as his chronic insubordination and countless service errors.

Social Information

So victims prematurely develop sinister explanations and then set out to confirm those explanations—and they do not do this in social isolation. Rather, their explanations often get reinforced by the people they talk to. Our data reveal that quite often victims discuss their feelings and hypotheses surrounding the offenders' actions in the company of other people, often coworkers. Calvin Morrill, in his work on conflict among executives, systematically observed workplace social gatherings whose purpose is to discuss managerial mistakes and wrongdoings, which he labeled "bitch sessions."[38] Barry Goldman, in his studies on EEOC claims filed by terminated employees against their former employers, also showed the effect of the opinions of friends and family. He found that a strong determinant of whether claims were filed was the process by which attorneys and family members discussed offenses with the victim.[39]

These sessions of social venting open up the attribution process to group dynamics such as conformity and groupthink. When unsure of the true nature of causality, the victim may adopt the group's opinion—more so when the group has consensus.[40] Simply, when we are unsure about something, we are more likely to think what everyone else thinks (or says they think), whether they're wrong or right. As a result, these sessions may produce an illusion of consensus, if only in the victim's eyes. That is, if we check with a few of our coworkers, who express the same negative opinion, we assume that *everyone* at work shares that opinion. Although employees may make good intuitive *jurists*, they can make lousy intuitive *scientists*—that is, unlike social scientists (and professional pollsters), too few employees consider the size and location of their sample of opinions, not realizing that such a small sample, and one that is not drawn at random (not *even close* to random!), can never tell them what everybody thinks.

Alternatively, while out collecting opinions, just a few opposing opinions—that the offender's motives really are benign—may be enough to convince the victim not to make sinister attributions. In experiments on social conformity, the presence of only a small percentage of dissenters was enough to change the subjects' opinions and actions.[41] Explanations and justifications by offenders may have a similar impact on muting the desire for revenge.[42]

When victims are actively seeking information, to whom do they turn? Do they turn to their friends, who know them well but may or may not know the offender well? Or do they turn to the offender's friends? The offender's friends may be the best source for information because they most likely have the best access to the offender's actual thinking. Better still, why not just ask the offender? Many victims do not ask the offender for a variety of reasons, including that they don't believe the offender will answer truthfully, or they find it too uncomfortable to approach the offender, perhaps because the victims prefer to avoid direct conflict or because an offender's higher status (say, as a boss or professor) makes the offender seem unapproachable.

Think back to the story of Sherry and Professor Ted. When Jim questioned Sherry about how she *knew* that every student in class thought Professor Ted was awful to her, she told him that she had talked about it with classmates in her group project. She said that they all thought Professor Ted was awful to her, and sometimes to them, too. And Jim did also hear complaints about Ted independently from other students in that class—but, interestingly, from only the students in Sherry's group project.

During this entire period, however, Sherry refused to talk to Professor Ted directly about any of these claims that so dramatically involved and affected him and her.

In general, many victims do as Sherry did and turn to their own friends and family for information.[43] Not only do victims often wish to avoid the offender and the offender's friends, they may also believe their own friends will provide much more sympathetic emotional support than the offender's friends would, and certainly than the offender would. Unfortunately, friends often tell friends what they want to hear, and even when they don't, the victims may *hear* what they want to hear: "Yes, he's the sinner, you're the saint." It is quite easy to confuse emotional support for cognitive agreement, and thus perceive confirmation when none exists. Even worse, perhaps, within their own group of friends and coworkers, the victims may seek out those who most dislike the offender, who may be very willing to confirm any opinion critical of the offender. Thus, victims may find more reinforcement for their early, suspicious attributions than is at all justified.

Biased Punctuation of Conflict History: Who Started It?

Revenge often is not just a one-shot affair that ends when the victim gives the offender just desserts—especially when the offender doesn't see the revenge as just. All too often the victim and offender don't tell the same story of their conflict. They don't even agree who has the victim role and who has the offender role. Much like the Princeton and Dartmouth football fans, they don't even see the same conflict and thus can't tell the same story.

At the core, the problem with revenge is that it invites counterretaliation. While the victims-cum-avengers may believe they have evened the score for the harms that befell them, the offenders-cum-targets may disagree. The offenders instead may see the revenge act as the only harm, or the bigger harm, and thus believe that to truly even the score, they must strike back.

Thus a one-shot conflict can escalate into a feud. It does so, in part, because of another bias—the *biased punctuation of conflict history*—that stems from the rest of the biases. This bias refers to a tendency for individuals to construe the history of conflict with others in a self-serving fashion.[44] Specifically, each individual misremembers a continuous, protracted history of conflict by mentally breaking it up into discrete acts of aggression—much as periods or commas break up or punctuate a long continuous stream of words into discrete, understandable sentences and phrases. But in a two-party conflict, such punctuation is biased and self-serving: each party believes the other started the conflict and is responsible for its escalation. Hence, there are always two sides to every feud (or three—see the following box).

Three Sides to Every Story

In his song "Long Way Home," Don Henley sings, "There's three sides to every story, baby: yours, mine and the cold, hard truth." Henley, a member of the country rock group The Eagles, knows something about feuds. Things got so heated among the band members that during the group's last concert in 1980, between songs, group members Glenn Frey and Don Felder threatened to punch each other out when the concert finished. After the tour, the Eagles still owed their record company, Warner Brothers, one more album, but because they could not stand to be in the same studio together, they mixed *The Eagles Live* from two different coasts, shipping tracks back and forth via courier. The album thanked five attorneys in the liner notes. Henley repeatedly said the Eagles would reunite "when Hell freezes over." The footnote to this story? Fourteen years later, they reunited—and named their reunion the "Hell Freezes Over" tour.

Observers of conflict also can be affected by the biased punctuation of conflict history. Often, observers see only part of the story. They see the retaliatory aggression, but not the first aggression that provoked it—thus viewing the retaliation simply as unprovoked aggression. For example, consider referees who officiate at professional sports events such as football and hockey games where fistfights often break out. The referees rarely see who threw the first punch, but they do see who threw the second one and consequently penalize only that second player. Ideally, to serve justice, the referees would see the whole conflict, from beginning to end, and thus penalize both players or neither.

Consider too the example found in the story of the mutiny on the *Bounty*. After the mutiny, the British court tried Roger Byam on charges of mutiny. The court saw mutiny as the only crime, the only provocation that must be punished. The court perceived the whole conflict as starting with the mutiny. But Roger Byam, punctuating the history differently, saw that the conflict started before the mutiny: it started when Captain Bligh abused the crew of the *Bounty*. Thus, Byam said in his defense, "I do not try to justify [Fletcher Christian's] crime, his mutiny, but I condemn the tyranny that drove him to it." Thus, by implication, Roger Byam felt that Captain Bligh also should be on trial, for it was Bligh's mistreatment of the crew that motivated their mutiny. (For a detailed illustration and diagram of a biased punctuation conflict, see the following box.)

Biased Punctuation of a Tit-for-Tat Feud

An employee named Eric and his manager, Melinda, become engaged in a feud, as follows: On Monday, Eric ignores Melinda's most recent request. Tuesday, Melinda reprimands Eric for poor performance on a recent task, publicly, embarrassing him. Wednesday, he actively avoids her, knowing that she needs his help on a task that day.

Thursday, she lets Eric know that she has recorded in Eric's file her impression of his lazy work habits that week, and will discuss it formally at performance review. Friday, Eric bad-mouths Melinda around the office. The following Monday, Melinda hears of the bad-mouthing, and assigns Eric an unpleasant task ... and on the conflict goes.

Let's diagram this conflict here to better understand precisely why biased punctuation is so insidious. Specifically, let's diagram it as:

.... E-M-E-M-E-M-E-M-E-M-E-M-E ....

where "E" means Eric did something nasty to Melinda, and "M" means that Melinda did something nasty to Eric. The ellipsis to the left represent that his feud has gone on for some time in the past, and the ellipsis to the right represent that the feud will go on in the future. Here we see a string of tit-for-tat aggressions by Eric, then Melinda, then Eric, then Melinda, then Eric, and so on.

If this diagram represents the "cold hard truth," what might the conflict look like from Eric's biased point of view? First, let's presume Eric doesn't remember how long the conflict has gone on. So, he sees only the part of the conflict represented in the shaded part of the diagram:

.... E-M-E-M-E-M-E-M-E-M-E-M-E ....

Next, suffering from a biased punctuation of the conflict history, Eric places punctuation marks—commas—as follows:

.... E-M-E- M-E, M-E, M-E, M-E, M-E, ...

Now look at the conflict from Melinda's biased point of view. Suppose that she remembers the conflict beginning a little further back than Eric does—and she places her own biased punctuation marks accordingly:

.... E-M, E-M, E-M, E-M, E-M, E-M, E ....

In summary, we have three sides to the story:

Cold Hard Truth: .... E-M-E-M-E-M-E-M-E-M-E-M-E ....

Eric's Story: .... E-M-E-M-E,M-E,M-E,M-E,M-E, ...

Melinda's Story: .... E-M,E-M,E-M,E-M,E-M,E-M,E ....

So if we were to ask Eric and Melinda separately to explain the cause of the feud, and each is punctuating the conflict with a self-serving bias, we would expect each person to blame the other for the conflict. Specifically, Eric the employee, $\underline{E}$, would reinterpret the history of the feud with his manager, Melinda, $\underline{M}$, as a sequence of exchanges $\underline{M\text{-}E}$, $\underline{M\text{-}E}$, $\underline{M\text{-}E}$, $\underline{M\text{-}E}$, in which the initial hostile or aggressive move was made by $\underline{M}$. That is, on Tuesday, Melinda "started it" by reprimanding him. So, on Wednesday, Eric withholds help. Then on Thursday—totally unprovoked (because the score was evened on Wednesday)—Melinda makes a critical recording in Eric's performance file. Thus, on Friday, Eric gets even by bad-mouthing Melinda. Then, on Monday, totally unprovoked again (!) (because the score was even after Eric's last action), Melinda hurts Eric by assigning an unpleasant task. In short, from Eric's perspective, all of his actions are *reactions*—they are legitimate and proportionate responses to malicious, provocative acts by Melinda.

However, Melinda punctuates the same history of interaction between them quite differently—as $\underline{E\text{-}M}$, $\underline{E\text{-}M}$, $\underline{E\text{-}M}$, $\underline{E\text{-}M}$, in which the roles of "offender" and "responder" are reversed. For her, their conflict began on the first Monday, when he ignored her request. It was on Tuesday, when she reprimanded him for poor performance the week before, that the score was evened. When Eric avoided her on Wednesday, that action struck Melinda as unprovoked, because the score was even the previous afternoon. Thus, from Melinda's perspective, each of Eric's actions is an unprovoked misbehavior or attack, while each of her actions is a legitimate and proportionate response.

In summary, because Eric and Melinda tell—and see— two different stories, neither of which is exactly the cold hard truth, they are doomed to continue feuding as long as they both continue to respond tit for tat.

In terms of its role in the cause of revenge behavior, the importance of biased punctuation of conflict history is fourfold. First, it allows justification of one's motives for aggression. As J.D. Frank perceptively notes, construing the history of conflict in this way can be used to justify the claim that one needs "to defend against a powerful and evil enemy, *thereby shifting responsibility for one's own aggressive actions to the opponent.*[45] In our research, we found a similar justification for revenge behavior by avengers, who viewed their actions as "morally right" and "in service of justice."[46]

Second, biased punctuation of conflict tends to generate self-fulfilling patterns of action-reaction between the parties as each tries to restore balance to the relationship by evening the score.[47] In other words, both sides view their own actions as purely defensive behaviors made in response to the other's unwarranted, offensive actions.

Third, it suggests how dangerous it can be to respond tit for tat to the other party in a futile attempt to "even the score." Clearly, because of these biases, the parties are not using the same scorecard and thus will never at any point in time agree that the score is even. One party will always be behind, and thus looking to even the score through further aggression. And such feuding can lead to hatred, not only on the international stage between countries and nation-states[48] but also in the corporate mailroom—or boardroom.[49]

Fourth, the phenomenon of biased punctuation serves as a reminder that even though revenge behavior often appears to be a response to a specific precipitating event (say, a dismissal that is perceived as unjust), such acts are almost always embedded in a protracted history of perceived injustices or conflict.[50] In this regard, acts of revenge within organizations are seldom lightning bolts from a blue sky. Instead, managers and coworkers usually report, especially with the advantage of hindsight, that such acts followed a protracted history of behaviors and exchanges suggesting something was seriously wrong with the individual (muttering, withdrawal, veiled threats, and the like). From the perspective of outsiders, these events often seem minor and unrelated. In the avenger's mind, however, they form a coherent and cumulative pattern of egregious insult and injury, necessitating a *proportionate* retaliatory response against the organization or one or more of its members.[51] What seems to outsiders like a minor insult becomes perceived as the "straw that broke the camel's back" to the aggrieved avenger.[52] (See the following box.)

The War of the Roses

In the movie *The War of the Roses*, Michael Douglas plays Oliver, who is married to Kathleen Turner's character, Barbara. Their "war" begins with a long, slow simmer as Oliver ignores Barbara and the kids for years while working on his career as an attorney. Years later, as Barbara decides to build a career of her own, starting a catering business, their simmering conflict explodes into an all-out tit-for-tat brawl. For instance, when Barbara asks for a divorce, she uses a personal letter from Oliver where he credits her with his success, which he wrote when he thought he was dying from a heart attack. She felt this act was justified because Oliver had belittled her attempt to start a business. Oliver perceives the use of the letter as low-handed betrayal and the first shot, so he retaliates by moving back into their house that he had moved out of, just to annoy her.

Barbara, feeling his move-in was unprovoked aggression, then evens the score by going out of her way to be an uncooperative roommate (for example, she won't share aspirin). Oliver then accidentally runs over Barbara's cat, but refuses to show remorse. So Barbara retaliates by making Oliver believe she killed the dog, made pâté out of it, and served the doggie-pâté to Oliver. Oliver then ruins a dinner she put on for her catering clients. Barbara retaliates by destroying Oliver's car. And on it goes. Oliver and Barbara each believed that the other started it, and that the other was responsible for each level of escalation. Each strongly felt like the victim of the other's villainy. Each felt justified getting even. And if you've seen the movie, you know the over-the-top destruction that this war wrought in the end.

The ongoing conflict between Israelis and Palestinians offers a poignant case in point of such a tit-for-tat feud, according to reporters who have studied this conflict.[53] Palestinian terrorists send in a suicide bomber on a bus in retaliation for Israeli jet-fighter bombing of a terrorist headquarters, which was in retaliation for a Palestinian suicide bomber obliterating an outdoor café, which was in retaliation for Israel's shooting artillery shells into Gaza, which was in retaliation for a suicide bomber blowing up an open market, which was in retaliation for Israeli soldiers shooting . . . you get the idea. Each side sees itself as the victim and the other as the villainous aggressor.* Each side sees its acts as retaliation and the other's acts as provocations. Each

---

*Of course, each side consists of multiple parties and factions with different perspectives and agendas, some more aggressive or peaceful than others. Certainly, not all Israelis and Palestinians advocate a policy of retaliation. (For instance, see "Israeli tit-for-tat death claims," BBC.com, June 3, 2005). Nor would all such factions claim that both sides are equally victims and aggressors (for example, The Committee for Accuracy in Middle East Reporting in America, as exemplified in E. Rozenman, USA Today Editorial, August 22, 2003.) Finally, we do not mean to suggest that the Israeli-Palestinian conflict is nothing but a tit-for-tat feud; it is much more complex than that.

side believes it is sending the other the message "we will not be intimidated or trifled with; you will pay for your aggressions." And each side is getting *nowhere* with these actions. Rather than deterring the other side's aggression, as each side hopes its own acts of aggression will do, it encourages more aggression. Why? Because, in part, each side is biasing the conflict history in a self-serving fashion.

One final example comes from the rock group Pink Floyd. In the mid-1980s, Roger Waters left the group, declaring it a "spent force creatively." Upon Waters's departure, guitarist David Gilmour mentioned to Waters that he might take over the creative leadership of Pink Floyd, to which Waters uttered his famous parting shot, "You'll never f---ing do it."[54] That shot was just the extra motivation Gilmour needed,[55] so in 1987 he and a remaining band member, Nick Mason, decided to make an album, *A Momentary Lapse of Reason*, and go on tour as "Pink Floyd." Waters was appalled. How could the group call itself "Pink Floyd" without him? They could do so no more, he said, "than Paul McCartney and Ringo Starr could go out on tour and call themselves The Beatles,"[56] especially because Waters had written most of the music and all of the lyrics for Pink Floyd's previous five albums. Waters believed that calling the album and tour "Pink Floyd" was a lie and an injustice; in his mind, it was really a David Gilmour solo album and tour, and he decided to move aggressively to stop it. That is, he hired lawyers to get an injunction to stop Gilmour and bandmates Mason and Wright from using the name "Pink Floyd."*

Waters lost the suit, however, so he retaliated by bad-mouthing the group's efforts publicly, calling their album "a forgery."[57] They returned the bad-mouthing, referring to Waters as "a sourpuss" and dictator who'd made their lives hell in the last few years of working together. Waters retaliated by not

---

*This was not Waters's only reason to get the injunction to stop it, but it was one reason. Another reason, unrelated to our arguments here, had to do with terminating Waters's contract with Pink Floyd manager Steve O'Rourke.

letting them use the famous Pink Floyd concert prop of a large pig balloon without paying royalties to him, claiming that was his creation. That struck the band as petty and absurd, so to spite him they added balls to the pig balloon, thereby changing its sex, which got them out of paying royalties on it.

Out on tour at the same time, Waters tried to prove which one was really Pink by trying to put on a better show. Maybe it was the better show, maybe not; but his former bandmates delighted in selling out football stadiums while Waters had trouble selling out smaller basketball arenas. Waters then made note in nearly all of his public interviews that what sold out those football stadiums was the "brand name" of Pink Floyd, and not the current members of Pink Floyd or their recent musical efforts.[58] Moreover, he said that Gilmour, in regard to the Pink Floyd legacy, "had sold 'his child' into prostitution."[59] Gilmour of course told a different story, noting that he had spent his whole career building up the Pink Floyd identity instead of promoting his own name, and that just because one band member (Waters) didn't want to do it anymore didn't mean the rest of the band must give up. And so on it went, for almost twenty more years. Just like their friends, the Eagles, whenever a greatest-hits package or remix was done, they stayed thousands of miles apart, deciding tracks lists and mixes via lawyers and tapes sent via courier. This tit-for-tat feud lasted until 2005, when all of Pink Floyd (Gilmour, Mason, Wright, *and* Waters) decided to reunite for the Live 8 concert.

Mental biases and social influence shape one's perceptions of the harm done and how the blame is determined as a result. In addition, parties in a feud cannot keep the same scorecard. Indeed, they are unlikely to agree on who did what to whom, how bad or good it was, and who started it.

In the next chapter, we examine how these social and mental processes become the foundation of the emotions of righteous anger that fuels revenge in the workplace.

5

"I'M AS MAD AS HELL AND I'M NOT GOING TO TAKE IT ANYMORE!"

Understanding the Motivating Power of Righteous Anger

I have a right to my anger,
and I don't want anybody telling me I shouldn't be,
that it's not nice to be,
and that something's wrong with me because I get
angry.

—*Maxine Waters*

Beyond the triggers of revenge and the way victims perceive (or *mis*perceive) the reasons for those triggers, the model addresses the desire for revenge. In this chapter we explore the emotional center of this desire—righteous anger—and how that emotion motivates revenge.

Just a few decades ago, a popular view among scientists was that emotions only make decisions worse: emotions interfere with clear thinking, motivate irrational responses, and bias perspectives.[1] While emotions can have these effects, increasingly science is showing the positive effect of emotions on decision making.[2] For instance, anger can help decision making when it spotlights issues as urgent and important and thus motivates action.[3] The anger that motivates revenge can also have both positive and negative effects. As Chris Matthews phrased it in his book on politics, *Hardball:* "Revenge is the nitroglycerin of politics. In extremis, it can get your heart started again. Used improperly, it can blow your head off."[4]

If Chapter Four was about gaining greater insight into the "mind game" that sparks revenge, this chapter is about the "heart game" that fuels revenge. Of course, the emotions of the heart and the perceptions of the mind both, to be technically correct, occur inside the brain. It is inside the brain where thoughts and emotions combine to make decisions, including the decision to get even.

Recently, in the field of neuroeconomics (that is, the study of what is going on at the neural level when people make economic decisions) scientist Alan Sanfey and his team of researchers studied what happens neurologically when people decide to get even.[5] Perhaps not surprisingly, they found that negative emotions shape the decision to get even. To show this, they had subjects play the "ultimatum game," which is essentially a revenge game, while lying in a functional Magnetic Resonance Imaging (fMRI) machine. The fMRI machine shows which structures in the brain "light up," showing that they are involved in mental tasks such as decision making.

The ultimatum game is well known in the fields of behavioral economics, game theory, and negotiation. Here's how it works: Two people are given a fixed sum of money to divide, say, $10. One person, the proposer, gets to propose a split of the money; the other person, the decider, decides to accept or reject the split. Here's the catch: if the decider rejects the proposed split, *neither* person gets *any* money. Now, hard-core economists will argue that the rational solution to this ultimatum game requires proposers to maximize their own outcomes by offering deciders only slightly more than zero and taking everything else for themselves. Moreover, because even a very small amount of money is still more desirable than nothing, the deciders should accept such an offer.

It turns out, however, that people playing this game aren't as "rational" as hard-core economists expect. Instead, deciders will "cut off their nose to spite their face" by rejecting greedy proposals. Offers that allocate 80 percent or more for the proposer (and thus 20 percent or less for the decider) are usually rejected.[6] That is, the deciders get even (literally!) when proposers make such greedy offers, angrily saying (for example): "You offer me only $2 of the $10? Screw you! I'll gladly give up that $2 to make sure you get nothing!" Because most proposers can figure out that deciders would consider such uneven offers unfair and thus reject them, most proposers don't propose them. This is why the median division proposed is more even, around 60 percent/40 percent, and deciders usually accept this offer.[7]

So, how emotional versus cognitive is this decision to reject greedy offers? That's what Sanfey and his colleagues learned by having people play this game while lying in an fMRI machine. Each subject saw thirty offers believed to be from either another subject or from a computer. Some offers were even ($5 each), and some were uneven (up to $9 to the proposer and $1 to the decider). When subjects received even offers from persons, or any kind of offer from the computer, the brain area that lit up was the dorsolateral prefrontal cortex (DLPFC), where thought, but not feeling, occurs. Thus, even offers and computer offers gave subjects something to think about, but not much to feel about. When subjects saw uneven offers from people, however, then not only the DLPFC lit up but also the anterior insula region of the brain, which is associated with negative emotion. As Sanfey's group concluded, "The areas of anterior insula and DLPFC represent the twin demands of the Ultimatum Game task, the emotional goal of resisting unfairness and the cognitive goal of accumulating money, respectively."[8]

So, there we have it: scientific proof that people can get angry at unfair offers, and may make decisions to get even while angry. Perhaps you already suspected that; we did. But it is always good to have an expectation validated through scientific method. This study, and a rich literature on aggression, show that injustice often generates anger, which leads to revenge.[9] But what we did *not* know until we interviewed people was, Why does such anger in revenge so fascinate everybody? What exact shape does that anger take? Are people annoyed, disgusted, or outraged? And exactly how does such anger motivate revenge?

A Primal Response

Perhaps the one aspect of revenge that fascinates people most is the human and primal nature of the heartfelt anger motivating revenge. Intense emotion makes revenge dramatic, and such drama draws attention to the victim, even before the victim strikes back. Perhaps this intense, dramatic anger is one reason that revenge fiction sells so well. But aside from those extreme kinds of stories, there are the harms and wrongs that happen on an everyday basis, the types of events that ordinary people can imagine themselves experiencing and doing as a natural, human response. Indeed, many people identify with the words of the painter, Paul Gauguin: "Life being what it is, one dreams of revenge."

But while we find the emotions that drive revenge fascinating, we are fearful of them because passion and anger are often uncontrollable. When people are very angry, things can and do get out of hand. Perhaps this is why Sir Francis Bacon described revenge as "kind of a wild justice, which the more man's nature runs to, the more ought law to weed it out." It may not be the justice part of wild justice that people mind as much as the wildness of the emotions that motivate that search for justice.

A good depiction of both the fascination and fear of revenge was in *Network*, which won four Oscars in 1976. In the movie, Howard Beale (played by actor Peter Finch) is fired from his job as anchor of the evening news, but is allowed on the air one last time to give a dignified farewell. Instead, he takes the opportunity to get even, exclaiming on air, "I'm as mad as hell and I'm not going to take it anymore!" Although the situation frightens management, it so fascinates the public that the news show's ratings skyrocket and Beale's angry exclamation becomes a popular catch-phrase that unleashes the viewers' anger at the world. And then the situation gets out of hand as Beale spreads his populist message of anger and the network reorganizes itself to take advantage of Beale.

While fear and fascination may make people ambivalent about revenge, our research has shown that to understand and predict revenge, we must focus on the anger that motivates it—a *righteous* anger, an anger that has a moral foundation. It is the righteousness of the anger that justifies the thinking about, if not the acting out, of revenge. One of the most vivid illustrations of this emotion that we've seen was depicted in a movie from the 1980s called 9 *to* 5.

9 to 5

The movie focuses on three women, Violet Newstead (played by Lily Tomlin), Doralee Rhodes (Dolly Parton), and Judy Bernly (Jane Fonda), who work for a "sexist, egotistical, lying, hypocritical, and bigoted" boss, Franklin Hart Jr. (Dabney Coleman). Each of these women experiences a sense of injustice as a result of her dealings with Mr. Hart, which is the source of revenge fantasies that ultimately lead to getting even with him.

For example, Violet becomes angry when a man is promoted ahead of her to a job that she clearly deserved but was denied because she was a woman. Upon hearing the news, Violet's first stunned response is: "*What?!*" When Mr. Hart offers his prejudiced explanation, Violet responds with words grounded in the emotions of righteous anger: "I've got five years seniority [over him] ... and I trained him!" she says. "I've been working my butt off at this company.... I'm losing a promotion because of some idiot prejudice.... Okay, don't ever refer to me as 'your girl.' I expect to be treated equally and with a little dignity and a little respect."

As Violet leaves Hart's office, she informs Doralee, who just entered the room, that she knows that Doralee is Hart's mistress.

When Doralee asks Violet who told her that, Violet points to Mr. Hart. Like Violet, Doralee instantly responds with a stunned, "*What?!*"—and she is similarly offended and outraged by the boss's actions. Listen for the emotions of righteous anger that ripple through Doralee's response:

> That explains it … that's why everybody treats me like some "dime store floozy." They think I am screwing the boss…. Look, I've been straight with you from the first day I got here. I put up with your pinching, staring, and chasing me around the desk because I need this job. But this is the last straw. Look, I gotta gun out in my purse, and, up to now, I've been forgiving and forgetting because that's the way I've been brought up. But I'm going to tell you one thing … if you ever say another word about me or make another indecent proposal, I'm going to get that gun of mine and I'm going to change you from a rooster to a hen with one shot. Don't think I can't do it! I never thought I'd live to say this about another human being, but you are evil, that's right, EVIL TO THE CORE!

The movie *9 to 5* is all about revenge and what drives people to try to get even. And as some of the dialogue illustrates, the emotions of righteous anger are central to the motivation for revenge. Although the movie appears to depict a humorous take on the everyday experiences of people in the workplace, in reality, the emotions and the actions that trigger them are not that funny. (For another example, see the following box.)

Tucker: The Man and His Dream

The true story of Preston Tucker, entrepreneur and innovator, was chronicled in the movie *Tucker: The Man and His Dream*. Just after World War II ended, Preston Tucker designed "the car of the future." This ground-breaking car had numerous innovations that the Detroit automakers had never imagined, such as seat belts, disc brakes, fuel injection, and a rear engine. When the car began to capture the imagination of the American public, the Detroit automakers felt threatened—and with the help of Senator Homer Ferguson of Michigan, they began efforts to stop Tucker.

Meanwhile, Tucker needed financial capital to build his cars. So Abe Karatz, Tucker's attorney—in an effort to signal the investment community of Tucker Auto Company's legitimacy—signed on a respected auto executive, Robert Bennington, to "run" the company. When Bennington began to make changes to the Tucker auto (to make it look more like traditional Detroit autos), Preston Tucker decided to confront the board of "his" company.

As depicted in the movie, when Tucker begins to speak, Bennington asks him to leave the board meeting, since he (Bennington) now runs the company. Tucker, looking stunned, asks Karatz if what Bennington said was true. Karatz informs Tucker that he had essentially given over the company to Robert Bennington in Bennington's contract, in return for Bennington's name to raise stock. Hearing this news, Tucker hits the table with his fist and says angrily: "This is MY company, Bennington! That means seat belts, disc brakes, fuel injection, and a rear engine!" Bennington responds: "We'll see about that, Mr. Tucker."

Tucker returns home and, still angry, throws the telephone against the wall, yelling: "That sonofabitch is not going to take over my company!" His daughter tries to calm Tucker down, but the visceral—and righteous—anger is still evident. At that moment, Tucker receives a phone call from Howard Hughes, who agrees to help Tucker. Tucker needed steel, and Hughes wanted to help Tucker because Hughes had been subpoenaed by Ferguson's Senate committee in which he had to show up or go to jail. With Hughes's help, Tucker now channels his righteous anger into getting even by building his car. In this way, Tucker's story is similar to that of Data General's Tom West, recounted in Chapter One. That is, Tucker was motivated not only by the desire to help his firm succeed but also by the desire to get even with Bennington and the board of directors.

Let us move now from the "reel life" of movies to the real life of the workplace.

Taking It Personally: Three Stories

John, a senior executive in a media and entertainment company, had for years been very successful developing creative and innovative offerings that had done very well in the marketplace. People in the company saw John as a visionary, someone who could see into the future and put together projects that really stimulated and excited the public. As a result, he had been given considerable freedom to create and break new ground with innovative product offerings. Members of John's team felt they were part of something extraordinary.

But with a change in leadership at the head of the company, John's professional life was about to take a dramatic turn. The new CEO was a dictator who specialized in micromanagement. The CEO was hell-bent to change every aspect of the organization and how it operated, and he could fire those who got in his way. Because he wanted total control, he particularly didn't like people who had freedom, so over a period of several months the new CEO slowly took away John's autonomy. As part of this cultural revolution, the institution was ever-so-slowly being remade in the image and values of the CEO while creating a reign of terror for those who worked there.

While the CEO continued to undercut John, he also realized that he needed John to keep the creative and innovative product stream alive. To remind John who was in charge, the CEO offered

John a new contract in which he expected John to do more in terms of output, but at half of the compensation. Indignant at this offer, John got even by resigning.

The CEO, stunned because nobody had ever stood up to him before, then retaliated by bad-mouthing John to other senior executives, even fabricating stories about John's motives for resignation. Even though John had left the company, these lies were damaging his reputation among his old colleagues, and John was furious. In his own words: "[The CEO] is a pathetic old man, one who thrives on instilling fear and terror in the hearts and minds of people. But not me. I am not afraid of him, which I know galls him," he continued. "But that doesn't mean I'm not angry and that I won't get even. I will gut him like a fish I just caught. My anger sustains me, keeps me vigilant, looking for *all* of the opportunities to make this 'poor excuse for a human being' receive justice. And trust me, justice will be served on a silver platter!"

You can clearly hear John's anger in his words, anger targeted at the CEO, whom John explicitly—and vividly—blames. That anger and blame create a "righteous anger" that is at the core of the sense of injustice that John is clearly expressing.

Similarly, consider the story of Elizabeth, a consumer products executive who worked for another petty tyrant. Elizabeth was one of the best at her job in this global company. But her boss believed he was the greatest and the most brilliant of all executives. So he micromanaged and publicly criticized Elizabeth and her team, often bringing members of her team to tears. As Elizabeth described her feelings about this boss: "I hated him. I busted my *!# for him, but it was never good enough. Some days I would just seethe. But then I realized that wouldn't be good enough, as I wanted to bring him down in a ball of flames. My team and I didn't deserve to be treated this way, nobody did. My anger was burning me up inside and I wanted him to 'feel my pain' and the pain of every other person he terrorized."

Again, the righteous anger in Elizabeth's words comes through loud and clear. And that anger is targeted at her boss. One can almost feel the heat behind her words—and the intensity of the anger ready to be acted out in revenge, which is what Elizabeth did. Using her contacts at corporate, she arranged for an outside coach to come in to evaluate the situation. The boss was told that if it was him or her, she would prevail. He had to mend his ways or else!

Then there is the case of Tina, a first-line supervisor in the customer care group of a large hotel located in the eastern United States. Tina led a team that had developed a reputation for being the gold standard in terms of providing the fastest—and most effective—response to corporate clients when they expressed dissatisfaction with their experiences with the hotel. Tina was proud of the team's success and credited her team for being so creative and responsive in handling corporate client complaints.

But things changed when a new department head arrived. This head was on a mission to run a leaner customer care group for the hotel so that he could look good to hotel management. That mission translated to Tina losing two members of her team to layoffs. Tina complained that these losses would compromise the quality and effectiveness of the customer care that her team provided corporate clients. Tina was outraged when her real concerns about compromising the quality of customer care fell on the department head's deaf ears.

So what did Tina do? She and her team stopped caring. While they were still responsive to corporate clients, they did not respond as quickly as they had in the past. The corporate clients could tell the difference in customer care and voiced their concerns to the hotel management. Hotel management blamed the department head for this growing dissatisfaction of corporate clients. As Tina said: "I was angry. I wanted customer care to fail so that the new department head would fail. What he had done was so wrong. It was sinful."

As in the previous examples, there's no mistaking Tina's anger—the righteous anger—in her words, nor Tina's desire to get even with the new department head.

These examples all share several common themes. First, anger was expressed, and more specifically, a righteous anger. Second, this righteous anger was targeted at someone who was to blame. Third, that anger created a desire or motivation to act. Fourth, as described, the emotions were intense; they captivated the people—psychologically and physiologically—as they experienced the event. Finally, in each of the examples, the victims took the harm or wrongdoing *personally*, as if it was an attack on them.

The Emotional Landscape of Revenge

What we have discovered in our research is that righteous anger is a complex emotion with different dimensions. And each dimension provides clues to the desire and motivation for revenge. One of these dimensions focuses on a sense of violation—*violation of expectations* and *violation of a sacred trust*. The second dimension focuses on *intensity* and *tyrannical quality*—the pain of the emotion and how it is experienced.

Sense of Violation: Expectations and Sacred Trust

One way that people experience a sense of violation regards a *violation of expectations*. As in the movie 9 *to* 5, one thing that triggers a righteous aspect to the anger is that the harm came as a surprise to the victim.[10] The victim simply didn't see it coming, and thus victims often report feeling confused or stunned by the harm. As a team leader in a financial services company described it to us: "I couldn't believe what had just happened. When he attacked me in front of my coworkers, I was paralyzed and speechless." Note that across scores of our interview subjects, the harm they endured came as a surprise.

Victims are usually more than just stunned and mad, however; they moralize about their experience—and that's where the feeling of *violation of a sacred trust* comes into play. They weren't just hurt, they were *wronged*. And that wrong is viewed as a violation of trust. Consider the words of an administrative assistant in a consumer products company: "I could not believe that she changed the criteria for promotion, just to make sure 'her' person got the new job. I had trusted her up to then. I now know she has no honor. As a manager, you have a duty and an obligation to do the right thing. You may call me naive for believing that. I call myself a person who is honorable."

That sacred trust has two subdimensions. First, we expect our leaders and coworkers to conduct themselves with integrity in terms of adhering to norms and values, as discussed in Chapter Three. Thus, for example, leaders and coworkers should follow the rules and norms, and they should value the greater good of the organization over their own personal career interests. When leaders appear to violate rules and norms in pursuit of self-advancement, we refuse to trust them. Second, we expect our leaders and coworkers to treat us with dignity, where they view us not as a means to an end but as an end in ourselves. When we feel used or abused, it adds a sense of righteousness to our anger. We have a sense of self that we view as sacred. As one manager in a financial services company described the emotion: "He betrayed my confidence by sharing secrets that he said he would never share. My world was shattered. What I assumed to be sacred and true—the trust of a friend—was violated, if not destroyed forever."

The sense of a violated dignity—or sacred self—is found in the story of Jane, a middle manager at a U.S. federal agency. After being publicly criticized in a demeaning fashion by her boss, Jane described her feelings as follows: "I am a human being. I don't deserve to be treated like some subhuman species. He stripped me of my dignity to make a point. What point? That he is some macho man who is in charge and all-powerful? I hate him for what he did to me. I will never be the same."

All these examples show how the kind of anger that motivates revenge has a depth and moral foundation. Whether it is a violated expectation or a sense of sacred trust, people feel and experience such righteous anger deeply, and that makes it more difficult to manage. And the pain itself varies along two dimensions: intensity, and what's been described as the tyrannical quality of the pain.

Pain: Intensity and Tyrannical Quality

Victims often describe the *intensity* of the emotions they experience. The intensity reveals a strong visceral response of physiological and psychological pain. In fact, the initial emotions are often described as *white hot*, *furious*, or *bitter*, words that are clear expressions of pain, anger, and rage. A middle manager in a consumer products company described herself as "inflamed and enraged," and "consumed by thoughts of revenge," while another middle manager in a global defense and aerospace company described the need to satisfy the "burning desire" for revenge.

The intensity of the pain is not just psychological—it is also physiological. Many people in our studies report a variety of symptoms including uncontrollable crying, knots in the stomach, and physical exhaustion. Based on these findings, it is clear that the righteous anger is an intensely *felt* experience. Consider the following words of a lower-level manager at an information products company, speaking about his boss: "His actions are so mean-spirited. He calls us names in meetings. His relentless criticism hurts us deeply. Each day at work, we feel sick to our stomachs. We feel like victims of 'emotional violence.' Why does he abuse us like this?"

And consider the description of intense emotions from a project manager at a Fortune 500 company: "I was so angry. He betrayed me, he used me. With each second I could feel the pressure building inside of me. I could feel the rage in my veins, pulsing, pushing me to get even."

But the emotional pain of righteous anger can also have a *tyrannical quality*, a psychological and physiological stranglehold on the individual. Consider the following examples, beginning with a senior manager at a consumer products company, recounting a terrible experience at work: "There are days I don't think about it, and in fact, I consciously try to focus on happy thoughts. But then someone will remind me of what happened and my anger and bitterness will just break through, overwhelming me like a hot flash. Despite my efforts to control my feelings, they just overtake me."

Consider a similar description from a first-line supervisor at a global telecommunications company, talking about her boss: "I am letting it 'eat' at me. I hate him for what he did to me, I really do. The mere thought of him causes me heartburn, and I am constantly thinking about him," she continued. "Sometimes my colleagues find me mumbling to myself, and this causes them to worry about me. Each day, I live with knots in my stomach, resenting his very being. I want him to suffer . . . forever!"

And, consider this third example from a middle manager at an energy company: "He publicly berated me, humiliated me in front of the team," he told us. "I never felt so angry. I hated him, I wanted him to die. I lived with that hatred for months until it literally ate my insides out. At that moment, I realized that he had been victimizing me for all of those months as I obsessed with what he did to me."

Each of these examples demonstrates how righteous anger can take over one's mind, heart, and body. The emotion of righteous anger can endure over time, sometimes for days, even weeks and months, if not longer. Indeed, the emotion of anger can be like a social toxin for some people, poisoning their professional and personal lives over time. And, as we have found in our research, often the social support of coworkers who continually vent about the injustice helps keep the emotions burning.

The emotional landscape that shapes revenge is tricky territory indeed. When we drill down to a deeper understanding of emotions, we find that it isn't simply anger that motivates revenge; rather, it is *righteous* anger. The righteousness of that anger is grounded in the sense of injustice, which motivates the act of revenge.

Edmond Cahn described this well in his seminal book on legal theory, *The Sense of Injustice* (1949). Cahn asks: "Why do we speak of the 'sense of injustice' rather than the 'sense of justice'? Because 'justice' has been so beclouded by natural-law writings that it almost inevitably brings to mind some ideal relation or static condition or set of perceptual standards, while we are concerned, on the contrary, with what is active, vital, and experiential in the reactions of human beings."[11] Writing more than half a century earlier, Cahn anticipates what Sanfey and his colleagues found in their fMRI machines in 2003: the sense of justice activates the thinking part of the brain, while the sense of injustice activates the feeling part.

Moreover, for Cahn, justice is "not a state, but a process; not a condition, but an action." He adds, " 'Justice,' as we shall use the term, means the *active process* of remedying or preventing that which would arouse the sense of injustice."[12] He defines the sense of injustice as "the sympathetic reaction of outrage, horror, shock, resentment, and anger, those affections of the viscera and abnormal secretions of the adrenals that prepare the human animal to resist attack. Nature has thus equipped all men to regard injustice to another as personal aggression."[13]

Cahn's description of the sense of injustice, and its action focus, is what we describe in this book. It is the sense of injustice that we have found motivates most acts of revenge. But how do people actually act out their sense that an injustice has occurred? In the next chapter, we describe the many different ways that people can—and do—exact their revenge.

6

YOU STARTED IT—
BUT I'LL FINISH IT!

How People Get Even

You think I'll let it go, you're mad;
You got another thing comin'.

—*Judas Priest*

Sam worked as an assistant to a senior editor at a major news magazine. The senior editor depended on Sam for everything, from keeping his schedule straight and booking his flights to catching errors that the fact-checkers missed in his articles. Sam was really good at his job—too good, it turned out. When a copyediting position opened up at the magazine, Sam saw his chance to move into an editorial track. He took the magazine's copyediting test and passed it. All he needed was his boss's recommendation to clinch the job. But rather than support Sam, the senior editor told him that he didn't think he was ready for the responsibility. He cited the fact that Sam had worked at the magazine for only a year, and some of his work habits needed honing. Sam seemed to get a lot of personal calls at the office, and he tended to arrive late many mornings (even though Sam often made up the time by working into the evening). Sam suspected that his boss simply didn't want to lose his "great assistant" or go through the hassle of finding a replacement. Regardless, without the senior editor's recommendation, he couldn't be hired for the copyediting team. Sam was furious and began considering how he might get even.

So, what does an offended employee like Sam *do* with all that anger, outrage, and desire to get even? What he chooses to do, if anything, depends on a number of factors, including his personality and the level of power (or powerlessness) he feels in the organization. To begin, here's a continuation of the list started in Chapter Two of the many methods employees use to get even—from the relatively mild to the all-out destructive.

Small, Everyday Acts of Revenge

Here are the milder examples of workplace revenge that we have catalogued in our research: the fantasies, freeze-outs, refusals of help, quiet decisions to work slower, and vows to work harder.

Fantasies

Much revenge may begin with revenge fantasies, and fortunately, much revenge stops there. Sometimes the fantasy of revenge is enough, especially if shared with others. In the movie *9 to 5*, before Violet, Doralee, and Judy took action to get even with Mr. Hart, they shared their revenge fantasies with each other.

Violet's fantasy had a fairy-tale theme, in which she is dressed as Snow White and is surrounded by cartoon animal characters. When Mr. Hart asks for coffee, she pours poison potion from her ring into his mug, and when he drinks it cartoon-like steam pours from his ears before his desk chair ejects him out of the high-rise building to the traffic below.

Doralee's fantasy has a cowboy theme, in which she is the boss and Hart is the assistant—an exact role reversal. She gives him some of his own medicine by using suggestive and sexually offensive language—"You have a nice package, you should show it off," "Loosen up and take off your bow tie"—that ultimately ends with her using a lasso to hog-tie him into submission. Similarly, Judy's revenge fantasy has a game-hunting theme, in which Judy, dressed in hunting garb and holding a shotgun, sits waiting in Hart's office chair. When Hart arrives, she accuses him of being a "sexist, egotistical wart on the nose of humanity" and shoots at him like the target in a carnival "duck shoot" booth. The scene ends with his head mounted on a wall plaque.

In our research, many people reported satisfying their revenge impulses by fantasizing about the painful and sordid revenge they would inflict on the perpetrator, but with no intention of acting on those feelings. Sometimes such fantasies were shared with others, even with coworkers. Fantasizing serves as a coping response that allows people to blow off steam or vent the emotions associated with injustice. It may be that fantasizing allows victims to feel powerful, rather than powerless, thinking of the harm they could inflict.[1]

Consider the revenge fantasy of Brian, a software engineer. Brian enjoyed his job, as it was challenging and gave him considerable freedom and autonomy. Then he got a new project manager, a "control freak" (in Brian's words), who began to micromanage Brian. Seething over how he was now being treated, Brian shared this fantasy:

> It is late at night. My project manager is working late. I have redone the code on the security system. At my command, the door locks and the office lights start flashing on and off. My project manager begins to scream for help. I now introduce rap music through the air vents. Through the surveillance cameras in his office, I watch him cry like a baby, curled up in the corner, sucking his thumb. And what makes it even more beautiful, I am filming all this for a spot on YouTube.

And consider the details of a fantasy recounted by Kelly, a program manager at a consumer products company about a coworker who was always needling her in meetings:

> I have her strapped in a chair, and I say, "So, you always try to get under my skin and you think it is funny. Let's see how funny it really is when I get under your skin." I inject her with a needle that has a virus that will eat out her intestines. She writhes and screams in pain.

Interestingly, enjoying fantasies of revenge does not mean someone intends to seek it. What we have found in our research is that often the fantasy was enough for people.* In this way, revenge fantasies aren't all that different from most other fantasies in life—they can be fun to think about, even if one never intends to go through with them.

The Freeze-Out

When others offend us, often we choose to avoid them. Avoidance is, in part, about making ourselves feel better simply by removing the negative stimulus from our environment. That is, we prevent further offenses, plus we don't let the offender's presence serve as a painful reminder of the offense. But avoidance often is about more than making ourselves feel better off; it's also about making the offender feel bad. By giving someone the silent treatment (a classic tactic that couples use, married or otherwise!), we make the offenders feel guilty (we hope) for their offense. In doing so, we teach the offenders a lesson—that is, to not do it again.

Consider the example of Sara, who worked in a public auditing agency. A coworker, Ned, participates in a betting pool of coworkers who wager on which newly married employees would get pregnant first. One day, Ned approaches Sara and says, "I heard you were pregnant; James told me so." Sara felt that comment was at best inappropriate, especially for a coworker who must deal with the public and therefore should have more tact, and at worst was sexual harassment. So Sara froze him out. In Sara's words, "To get even, I was downright mean. I didn't acknowledge his presence, staring past him if we happened to pass in the hallway. If Ned had a question on an account I audited that he was trying to collect, yes and no answers sufficed."

Sometimes, the avoidance is temporary; once we feel we have made our point and have evened the score, we can forget about

---

*As noted in Chapter Two, however, fantasies can fuel revenge when the harm is personal (that is, an attack on one's identity) and people perceive that harm to be intentional, if not malicious.

it and get on with the offender. Sometimes, however, the offense is so severe and unjust that we no longer trust the offender at all, and so the avoidance is permanent. Consider the story of Connie, a project manager at an information products company. Connie had become the target of a "backstabbing" campaign by another project manager. When Connie found out about these actions, she vowed to avoid that project manager "forever ... plus one day." When the project manager walked past Connie, she ignored him as if he were invisible. Connie asked her staff to do the same—that is, to shun that project manager. Connie has never spoken to the project manager again, despite attempts by the project manager to talk with her.

Some organizations have institutionalized that shunning process of avoiding people who harm others or do wrong to others. For example, one major U.S. airline has built into its staffing system a procedure for coworkers to permanently avoid each other. Specifically, when flight attendants request which flights they will work, they do so in a computerized scheduling system, which happens to have data-entry fields in which they can name up to three other flight attendants—flight attendants with whom they prefer not to be scheduled.

Refusal of Help

Those who find it beneath them to seek revenge can still enforce the norm of reciprocity through inaction rather than action. Sure, such principled victims won't commit misdeeds, but many will omit good deeds. Specifically, they may not help offenders when the help is not part of the victim's required duties.

For example, consider the case of an employee, Gary, who had heard that a coworker, Erin, insulted his competence. For a while, Gary did nothing. Later, when Gary and the coworker had to work together on a committee that handled a $750,000 machine order, Gary got his revenge. Gary discovered that completing this order correctly and on time required the use of an updated list of materials. Gary obtained the updated list so he could do his part of the order correctly. But then, he decided not to forward a copy to Erin, who also needed it to do her part of the order correctly (though she didn't know she needed it, and, technically, it wasn't Gary's official responsibility to make sure Erin had the data she needed). The result? The order had errors and was delayed by three weeks. Management looked into it, and praised the competence of Gary's work while dressing down Erin for her errors.

Working Slower

Often when the offender is the boss, or is the organization as a whole, victimized employees just stop trying. They work only hard enough to not get fired, but no harder. Jonathan Franzen describes such employees in his investigation of the underperforming Chicago Post Office circa 1994. One employee in particular, Erich Walch, after suggesting many potential improvements to the way mail was processed and delivered, became frustrated, commenting to Franzen about his fellow mail carriers: "A lot of people get to the point where they say, 'I have done everything I can, so I'm going to do less. I will take out only first- and second-class mail. I will take out maybe an extra one or two bulk-rate letters. And I'll walk real slow. And there's always tomorrow."[2]

The Chicago mail carriers' response is an example of what organizational justice scholars refer to as the classic "inequity reduction response."[3] That is, people who believe they are not rewarded in proportion to their contributions, but that peers are getting proportional rewards, feel a need to increase the ratio of their rewards to their contributions and thus bring things into balance. They can increase this ratio either by increasing the employer's rewards or by decreasing their contributions to the employer. Ideally, they would increase the rewards—for example, ask for and receive a pay raise. Failing that, then they may decrease their contributions—for example, work slower.

For another example, meet Bill, who one summer pruned cherry trees in an orchard. He worked hard for a month, working six-day weeks. He looked forward to a much-needed and deserved day off on Sunday, for which he made plans. But on Saturday night, his boss informed him that he would be working Sunday, too. As Bill described the inequity: "I thought that I deserved a day off, and I was angry that I didn't get one. I was also bitter that I was not being paid a percentage of the profit, which was part of the job offer my employer had made. I felt that I was working more than I needed to, and being paid less than I should be." So Bill showed up to work on Sunday, but pruned the trees simply and quickly (cutting the branches close to the trunks instead of up high, which takes more time), even though he knew that meant that the trees would produce much less fruit. In fact, for the next week, he pruned all the trees this way, thus ensuring that he would finish on Saturday and not have to work another Sunday.

A popular variation on working slower and less competently is "working to rule," which unions sometimes use in disputes with management. Here, the employee deliberately follows the letter of the boss's instructions but not the spirit. For instance, disgruntled union workers might follow every possible safety procedure on the shop floor, no matter how outdated and extreme, which they normally do not do, knowing that it will bring production down to a crawl. Working to rule perhaps happens most frequently when the offense involves a micromanaging boss.

For instance, think back to the example from Chapter Two: the manager who, no matter how small the detail, demanded that his direct reports seek his approval before making a decision. His direct reports then worked to rule by complying with his request precisely—for *every* decision, no matter how small and no matter when it occurred, they consulted him, depriving him of sleep. They knew that he really didn't *mean* they should bother him about the super-trivial decisions, but that's not what he *said*. So they complied with what he said rather than with what he meant, knowing it would bother him.

Also consider the example of Diane, who was asked to train her replacement. Her replacement was a man who came from a country, he explained, "where women have a lower place, and as far as I'm concerned, should stay there." He added that he was sure that there was nothing Diane could tell or show him that he did not already know. So she did what he asked of her: she did not tell him how to do the job, she did not show him the statistical quality controls, the computer bar-coding program, or the marketing and sales ordering procedure that he had to maintain. She decided *not* to introduce him to the network of people in the factory he needed to know to help him in his daily tasks.

Working Harder

Sometimes, employees can get revenge not by working slower or less competently but by doing the opposite: working harder, faster, and better. As one of our interview subjects put it, "I was determined to work twice as hard, and take twice as long, if need be." This form of revenge usually followed an offense that damaged the victims' reputations as good employees. Consider the captain of a U.S. Navy destroyer whose ship suffered "simulated hits" in a war game, and who also had to endure the bragging of the fellow captain responsible for making those hits. In the following week's exercise, the destroyer captain soundly beat the braggart with "simulated heavy damage." He reported restoring the ship's reputation and improved the crew's self-esteem.

Also, take the case of Joyce, who consistently had the top sales numbers in her photographic mail-order unit. One month, the company changed its procedures, which resulted in much confusion and stress among the salespeople. Joyce did not like the confusion and stress that the new system created, and so she spent the next two months helping her coworkers learn the new system instead of working on her own sales. However, this lowered her sales to the worst in the unit. Upon seeing the sales data, her boss then berated her, doubting her ability to adjust, and threatened that she'd better increase her sales figures or he would fire her. The following month, she stopped helping coworkers and focused on her own sales, and was once again the top salesperson. In doing so, she not only saved her job but also regained her reputation as a competent, high-performing employee. Even more, she was also able to rub her boss's nose in her success, saying, "Ha! See, anyone can do it, it is just a matter of doing it!"

Some may argue that working harder is not really "revenge." But just because an act may have positive consequences, and may have multiple motives including pro-social ones, that does not mean that it cannot also have *revenge motives*. For instance, when employees work harder to regain their reputations, they not only hope to help their own careers, they also wish to show up and prove wrong their offenders, thereby causing the offenders some loss of face too.

Working harder to vindicate oneself can also occur at the highest executive ranks. In her cover story in *Business Week* on "Sweet Revenge," Jena McGregor tells the story of Millard "Mickey" Drexler, the CEO of Gap Inc., who after nineteen years on the job was forced out in 2002. As McGregor wrote:[4]

> Unlike most other CEOs, who walk out the door with millions in severance, Drexler left behind a hefty package and its noncompete restrictions. That decision allowed him to bag a job leading preppy retailer J. Crew Inc.... Since joining J. Crew, Drexler, 62, has hired at least two dozen executives away from his former employer. He has also launched a new brand called Madewell that, with prices below J. Crew's, could compete with Gap.... Drexler has insisted he is not motivated by revenge, but he has also said that anger over his departure "helps fuel my accomplishment now." Even if payback isn't an active pursuit, he's probably savoring the redemption.... In its most recent quarter, operating income increased 51% from the year before. Meanwhile, his successor at Gap, Paul Pressler, is experiencing steady drops in sales and may be exploring a sale of the company. "[Drexler's] parting at Gap now in retrospect is probably deeply regretted," Evan S. Dobelle, a former Gap board member [said].

The More Extreme Forms of Revenge

In our research, we found that many people went beyond the milder forms of getting even like fantasizing and working harder. In fact, in 84 percent of the stories we collected, the interviewee did go beyond the milder forms. Some people engaged in far more confrontational, even destructive, forms of revenge such as assigning what they happily called "shit work," tattling, quitting, getting people fired, taking resources, giving bad service, and initiating litigation.

Assigning Shit Work

Another classic inequity reduction response is to unload "shit work" on particular people as a way of getting even—that is, giving them the unpleasant but necessary jobs that nobody wants to do yet must get done. But to whom to give such nasty jobs? How about the peers whose reward-to-contribution ratios are much higher than one's own? One might dump the work, justifying the dumping with, "You make the big bucks, so you do it!"

We also find that many bosses use these assignments as readily available means of revenge and punishment. For instance, Aaron, who worked as a banquet server for a major hotel chain, had a problem coworker, Shelley, who was so competitive that she would steal supplies from coworkers' banquet rooms to better set up her assigned room. One busy night, Aaron was in charge of assigning cleanup duties, and he decided to put Shelley on trash-hauling duty, pairing her with a coworker whom Aaron knew Shelley disliked intensely. Aaron reported enjoying listening to Shelley complain about hauling the heavy, smelly trash!

This form of revenge by bosses may be especially popular in organizations where bosses have fewer reward and punishment levers to pull, such as in government agencies and union shops. Take public universities, for example. It is said that it's impossible to get rid of underperforming tenured professors, because tenured professors can't be fired, except for unethical behavior and neglect of teaching duties—something that's very difficult and time-consuming to document. So some department chairs get their revenge by assigning these underperformers extra committee work, unpopular courses to teach, and unpleasant times to teach those courses.

The same situation exists for all full-time employees in government agencies, who, once they pass the probationary period (usually the first six months of work), are as hard to fire as tenured professors. In these cases, bosses have to persuade underperforming employees to leave "voluntarily." Sometimes, such persuasion is accomplished through revenge—such as "slowly torturing" the employee with burdensome and disgusting work, as one of our respondents put it, until the employee *wants* to leave.

Tattling

Often it is not enough for the offender to feel the sting of revenge; some avengers want others made aware of the offense (and sometimes the revenge) as well. For example, one coworker accuses another of not doing the job, but not to the other's face. The coworker's first complaint went in a memo to the boss, criticizing the other coworker because "this jerk . . . needs to be taught a lesson." (For more on an interesting phenomenon in the tattling world, see the following box.)

Online Tattletales

The phenomenon of customers' complaining online about poor service experiences neatly illustrates the multiple motives victims have for tattling. In particular, the Internet provides new and increasingly better means to bad-mouth firms and customer-service representatives. Any customer, for instance, can post a product review on Epinions.com. Moreover, other sites exist to just log *negative* experiences, such as ConsumerAffairs.com and rippedoffreport .com. Finally, for the really angry and computer-literate customers, there's the option of building whole Web sites dedicated to just one firm that they hate (which is how sites like www.walmart-blows.com, www.BestBuySux .org, www.starbucked.com, and ComCastMustDie.com are born).

Yany Gregoire studies how and why customers get even with firms. In a recent survey, Gregoire found that the major reasons people post to such Web sites are not only to seek legal advice, but also to "make the firm pay."[5] Sometimes, it's a bit of all these reasons, moving from one reason to another as the conflict escalates. For instance, an upset customer may initially give a customer service representative a hard time (venting anger and attempting to shame the rep) simply because the customer believes (often mistakenly) it's possible to bully the rep into conceding to the demand for, say, a refund. If this doesn't work, then the customer may go online to bad-mouth the company. For instance, Melinda told us that at the bridal shop where she used to work, it was a frequent occurrence that mothers of the brides-to-be would use the threat of online bad-mouthing to coerce discounts on bridal gowns.

Surprisingly, online complaining has proven quite effective in some cases, particularly due to its viral impact. In a cover story for *Business Week* titled "Consumer Vigilantes," Jena McGregor details the story of the Web site ComCastMustDie.com.[6] She writes that Comcast customers who felt they did not receive adequate responses from the company about their complaints went online to this site to complain. The owner of the site reported that bloggers on his site say that Comcast reads these complaints and contacts the bloggers to remedy their complaints.

Unfortunately, by the time customers blog about a complaint, it already may be too late for the firm, as McGregor recounts in the story of Justin Callaway from Portland, Oregon, and his crusade against Cingular/AT&T. Calloway believed that a technical glitch in the cell phone system fried one of his computer speakers, which was hooked up to his cell phone. He discovered what the glitch was and that Cingular knew of the glitch, and was angered that Cingular never disclosed it. So he made a song and video, "Feeling Cingular," and posted it to YouTube, where as of this writing, it has been viewed almost 45,000 times. A month after posting the video, he received an unsolicited e-mail from the VP of e-commerce at AT&T, who offered to replace the computer speaker. Callaway refused the offer, telling McGregor, "It wasn't about the speakers anymore"; presumably, it was about warning others and teaching AT&T a lesson. To continue that lesson, he has filed a class action lawsuit against AT&T.

The story of Justin Callaway is consistent with what Gregoire finds in recent research on customers who blog: once a customer has exacted revenge through blogging, that customer is not coming back. Specifically, while the desire for revenge decreases over time after one blogs, the desire to avoid the firm increases. Given the resources firms put into attracting new customers (for example, cell phone companies offer all sorts of deals, like free phones, to steal customers from each other), this is a significant problem for firms.

Avengers can have several reasons to go public by tattling. One is to *seek help* from other parties who had been unaware of the offense. Another reason is to *damage the offenders' reputation*, just so it hurts them more. Also, sometimes it is necessary to publicize the offense so as to *warn others* about the offender. Last, we find that when their reputation is damaged, some people feel that the only place to *get back that reputation* is in public.

Seeking Help. One form of revenge that repeatedly appeared in our research is the end run—that is, where victims go above their boss's head to the boss's boss. This is what an internal auditor, Alan, eventually did. While accompanying his supervisor on audits of off-site locations, Alan noticed how frequently his supervisor performed personal errands even though he was still clocked in on company time. Alan first talked to his supervisor about the errands, but his supervisor ordered him not to worry about it, even though it put Alan's reputation in jeopardy. Finally, after one errand too many, one that took all afternoon, Alan felt compelled to go to his supervisor's boss, the accounting manager, and tell the whole story. Alan needed his supervisor's boss's help to get out of this bad situation.

Or consider the story of Mischa, who was a first-line manager in a consumer products company. One of her primary responsibilities was managing the department budget. But Darren, the division's budget officer, kept finding what he claimed were errors in Mischa's work. They actually weren't errors, but Darren just liked to pick on first-line managers to remind them who was in charge. Mischa grew angry that she could do nothing to Darren, except to correct these so-called errors.

After this treatment had gone on for six months, Mischa decided to take action by going to her boss. After hearing what had been going on, Mischa's boss, Jerome, went to Darren's boss, Mary, who also happened to be a friend of Jerome's. Jerome described to Mary what had been going on with Darren. Jerome also said he had talked with other executives at the company and discovered that Darren's treatment was not limited to Mischa; indeed, Darren had treated several other first-line managers similarly—and those people were all women and minorities. Jerome suggested to Mary that there could be a real HR issue here, one that would make Mary look bad. Mary thanked Jerome for the heads-up and then walked down the hallway and met with Darren behind closed doors. Thereafter, Darren changed his behavior completely and was no longer a bother to Mischa nor to the other first-line managers. Three months later he was transferred to another part of the company.

As another example, consider this story recounted to us by a congressional aide in one of our studies. A constituent called the office asking for help with the IRS and getting what she referred to as "her" refund check, but lied about her circumstances (she was not supposed to receive the refund checks she was receiving; her daughter was). When the aide discovered the lie, he went out of his way to report her real circumstances to the IRS, which no longer gave her the refund checks.

Damaging the Offender's Reputation. Another reason to tattle is to increase the embarrassment and shame an offender might feel. As noted earlier in the book, employees have been known to bad-mouth their employers. Traditionally, such bad-mouthing occurs socially in the cafeteria and in bars after work, where employees feel safe that they won't be overheard. Bad-mouthing may be more likely in situations where the victim is afraid to confront the offender, as when employees are afraid to confront their bosses, but often it occurs in addition to confronting the offender.

For example, we heard many reports of employees' using small private gatherings such as lunches and coffee breaks to demonize their bosses—vent their frustrations, assign blame, call the bosses names (such as "Beelzebub"). In one case, we heard of subordinates' using humor to ridicule their boss: they would hold initiation ceremonies for new employees after they'd had their first abusive encounter with the boss. We also heard about a group of Louisiana coworkers who hated their abusive boss so much that they spent weeks planning a party in her "honor"—a voodoo ritual party where they shared stories and made doll and piñata effigies of the boss that they poked and batted.

Warning Others of Danger. Often, victims go public not merely to cause pain or seek help but also to reveal offenders so that other potential victims can be more wary. For instance, many online posts of troubles with firms include a warning, such as "don't buy from this firm or else you will experience poor service." In fact, eBay has a built-in warning system. After each transaction, both buyer and seller leave feedback about the quality of the transaction. If someone is dissatisfied with the transaction—for example, the buyer may not have paid promptly; the seller may have sold a broken item—then the unhappy party can leave negative feedback. Moreover, eBay makes easily visible the percentage and number of positive, neutral, and negative feedback reports each eBay user has received. The intent of this system is to warn potential eBay users about unethical or incompetent buyers and sellers. Interestingly, because dissatisfied buyers and sellers get even with negative feedback, people are *more* comfortable using eBay—this feedback system allows them to trust buying from and selling to complete strangers. In fact, regular eBay sellers cherish this feedback system so much that when eBay recently changed the feedback system so that sellers no longer could leave negative feedback for buyers, many sellers held a two-week-long "strike."

The eBay example is similar to the flight-attendant-scheduling system of the airline company described earlier. By providing the opportunity to shun specific flight attendants, it allows coworkers to signal to management about problem employees. That is, any flight attendant who repeatedly appears in other flight attendants' "do-not-schedule-me-with" field is a problem management must address.

Getting Back a Reputation. "Which office do I go to to get my reputation back?" This was the famous question that Raymond Donovan, former Secretary of Labor in the Reagan administration, asked after being acquitted of racketeering charges. His question was clearly grounded in the sense of injustice discussed in Chapter Five.

Moving from the courtroom to the workplace, apparently employees go to the "court of public opinion" to get their reputations back. That is, suppose someone attacks your reputation by putting you down in front of your peers. You now appear diminished in your peers' eyes (or worry that you appear so, not noticing that the offender looks like a jerk and your peers feel sorry for you). To regain your status and identity as a competent and trustworthy coworker, you therefore believe that you have to do something that your peers will see. It's not enough to prove to the offender that the attack was wrong, you also must prove it to your peers. So whatever you do to get even, you consider doing in front of them. Thus, if somebody unfairly criticizes you over -e-mail—including the whole department on the cc list—when you finally compose the perfect rebuttal, you click, not "reply," but "reply *all*."

This was the route taken by Casey, an industrial engineer in a large semiconductor manufacturing firm. Casey worked with Gary, whom Casey thought to be generally rude, obnoxious, lazy, and disorganized. At a project meeting with upper management, when Gary was asked about the status of his segment of the project, instead of apologizing for not completing it, Gary attacked Casey's leadership of the project, accusing him of poor planning and setting impossible goals. Casey began to plot his revenge. "I determined my method of revenge very tactfully," he said. "I knew the arena needed to be in a very visible forum." So at a later meeting, Casey prepared a detailed, polished report that included a pointed critique of the areas Gary supervised. "Gary took a lot of heat after that public roasting," Casey said, adding that thereafter, "Gary chose to treat me with utmost respect." (For more on how people attempt to regain their reputations, see the following box.)

Dueling Blogs

Appealing to the court of public opinion is even easier if you already have a public forum. Consider Michael Fremer, a writer for *Stereophile* and a columnist on the publication's Web site, who exacted his revenge against well-known public skeptic James Randi (a.k.a. the Amazing Randi). *Stereophile* is the leading reviewer of high-end stereo equipment for "audiophiles," who pursue the best-sounding stereo gear they can afford. James Randi is a former magician, now a scientific skeptic who challenges paranormal beliefs and pseudoscientific claims. A frequent guest on *The Tonight Show with Johnny Carson*, he once demonstrated that Uri Gellar could not really bend spoons with his mind. For years now, Randi has publicly offered a $1 million prize to anyone who can prove the existence of paranormal or supernatural phenomena, such as E.S.P., under scientific conditions. So far, he hasn't had to pay out the prize money.

Recently Randi added hearing differences among different brands of stereo-gear connecting-wire (such as speaker wire or patch cords) to the list of "phenomena" for which he would pay the famous prize. He scoffed at the idea that audiophiles, including the staff of *Stereophile*, could hear the difference between regular audio cables, such as $25 speaker wire, and boutique audio cables, such as $2,500 speaker wire (and that's the price *per foot!*). So Fremer took him up on the challenge, figuring it would be the easiest chunk of money he'd ever make. Fremer wrote in his regular online column, "I e-mailed Randi and told him I accepted his challenge. Why not? I'm pretty sure I can hear cable differences. No, I'd better be able to—if I couldn't hear cable differences under 'blind' conditions, I might just be the audiofool Randi had attacked me for being."

Fremer and Randi e-mailed back and forth, setting up the test conditions and deciding exactly which megabuck wire they would use. But after they'd settled on one brand of speaker wire, which cost $7,200, the manufacturer of that wire backed out, refusing to be the subject of the challenge. What riled Fremer, however, is that on Randi's Web site, Randi accused *Fremer* of backing out, which amounted to a public attack on Fremer's reputation. Fremer responded in kind—in public, posting a rebuttal on Randi's Web site and in Fremer's own column on *Stereophile's* Web site. As Fremer later recounted in his column, although Randi knew the manufacturer had pulled out, he nevertheless "disgustedly announced to his acolytes that he'd known that the 'blowhard' Fremer would never take the challenge, that the matter was closed, and that it was time to move on to the next challenger.... Randi had used [the manufacturer's] pullout as a cover for his own.... I immediately logged in to Randi's on-line forum and laid out the timeline to his worshippers.... I also called him a 'lying sack of shit,' which I thought accurate under the circumstances."[7]

Of course, as noted in Chapter Four, there are at least two sides to every such story. If you would like to make up your own mind about who really backed out, you can see for yourself. After all, it's all online!

Quitting

A very popular form of workplace revenge is to quit the job. Victims describe quitting not only as helping themselves, by getting them out of the bad situation, but also as revenge. They say it's revenge because they are also motivated to hurt their bosses or organizations. They believe that because their employers need them, their absence will disrupt the workplace, at least for a while. Moreover, some avengers hope that this disruption will teach their employers a lesson, such as, "If you treat your employees this way, they will leave."

Most abusive bosses don't make that connection; they don't see and, quite frankly, don't care how they treat employees. But enlightened leaders and managers are beginning to understand the economic value of treating people fairly and with dignity—specifically, that employees tend to quit jobs where they feel abused.[8] As one senior human resources executive told us: "People join an organization, but they leave a manager."

With that wisdom in mind, consider the story of Terry, a first-line supervisor at a retail store during the busy Christmas season. By the end of each day, the store looked trashed from all the customer traffic. So every night, the store operations manager, Paul, kept Terry and other employees locked in until 3:00 AM, well past the official end of their shifts, even though many of them had to report back to work a few hours later for the morning shift. Terry believed that Paul was a bully who "was doing this for selfish reasons (he was in charge of the warehouse) and that he didn't care about who he stepped on as long as his goals were met." So one night, against orders, Terry unlocked the doors and let the employees out early, that is, at 1:00 AM. The next day she was reprimanded and received a documented, verbal warning. Her reply? "Take your warning and shove it up your ass. Document that!" She quit on the spot, though she knew she was leaving the store without a warehouse supervisor at the busiest time of the year.

Sound familiar? Perhaps you remember the popular '80s song, "Take This Job and Shove It!" by Johnny Paycheck. His song may well be the anthem of people who exact their revenge by quitting.

Getting People Fired

Sometimes victims perceive particular offenses as so egregious that the offenders deserve to lose their jobs. So victims do what they can to have the offenders fired. In many organizations, bosses can fire employees on the spot. Coworkers, however, have to rope in a boss and persuade that boss that a coworker deserves to be fired. Take the case of Armando, who worked as a bank teller alongside Sandy. Although Armando knew that Sandy had a drug habit and was therefore unreliable, one week Armando had no choice but to ask Sandy to cover Armando's Saturday shift—and Sandy said he would. Come Saturday, however, Sandy did not show up and Armando's shift was left unfilled. Armando was fired. As part of his exit interview, Armando tipped off management about Sandy's drug problem, including times when Sandy did drugs at work. Management fired Sandy two months later after compiling enough evidence of his drug use, which they knew how to find thanks to Armando's tips.

Sometimes simply reporting the problem isn't enough; instead, one has to force the issue. Consider Geert, who worked for a small, family-owned company that operated as a distributor of farm equipment. When the company hired Erica as a new receptionist for the administrative office, Geert quickly concluded that Erica was not as skilled as she'd claimed to be in her interview. As Geert worked with her to implement an inventory tracking system, he criticized her performance, which made her cry, making her even more difficult to work with. Erica complained vocally and publicly about Geert's treatment of her, including revealing confidential information about Geert while bad-mouthing him after hours in a local bar. When Geert discovered that Erica borrowed money from petty cash for her personal needs, he complained to the company owners, but they did nothing about Erica. That's when Geert decided to force the owners to fire Erica, giving them the ultimatum, "She leaves or I leave." They fired Erica.

Taking Resources

One way to even the score, particularly for those who feel undercompensated, is to "find" more compensation. In our research, we found that this act of revenge ranged from using the office phone for private calls to charging lunches and dinners with friends as business expenses. Such behavior was viewed as "fair compensation" for harm endured by the victims. In a famous study of employee theft, Jerry Greenberg found that the amount of inventory and office supplies that employees stole was positively correlated with how much the employees felt underpaid.[9] Thus, sometimes, underpaid employees really do take home a few pens and pencils without feeling like they are stealing from the company.

Alternatively, employees may steal from each other, which is what Jack did. Jack's engineering firm hired a new engineer, Seth, who was to take over Jack's duties and office space as Jack moved up to a better project. The plan was for Jack to clean out his cubicle when he returned from his business trip. When Jack returned, he found Seth already occupying the cubicle, having stashed all of Jack's belongings in one corner of the cubicle. Jack told us, "What had been my personal space for the last three years had been completely violated by some newbie. Seth had completely made himself at home. I mentioned my frustration to Seth, but the only comment he could squirm out was, 'Sorry, guess you didn't move fast enough.' " So, when Seth was away from the desk, Jack not only removed his own belongings but removed three-fourths of the RAM from Seth's computer to put into his own new computer, even though he didn't really need more RAM.

Some employees (and many managers) consider wasting time at work as "stealing from the company." Employees may take extended coffee or lunch breaks, or the classic, use the computer to surf the Web or play solitaire. For instance, one employee we know, upset that her boss had borrowed her car all day when she had loaned it only for the morning, decided to play computer games all afternoon instead of working, in a deliberate effort to get even with her boss by wasting company time.

Giving Bad Service

We described earlier how customers get even with companies, but we also know of many ways that companies (or at least employees in those companies) get even with customers. In particular, customer service agents do not like rude customers. Frank Warren's "post.secrets" project, which is a Web site where anyone can anonymously post a deep but concise secret, illustrates a few examples of this. In fact, the quotation from the coffee barista that opened this book ("I give decaf to people who are rude to me") is from the post.secrets project. Another, perhaps more troubling, example we found on this site came from a hospital nurse, who confessed, "If a patient is rude to me or mean to his family, I use the largest gauge needle I have to inject him. If a patient is nice, I use a baby needle."

In a study of hotel and restaurant service in New Zealand, Vicky Browning of the University of Otago found that front-line employees very much react to customers who are rude, argumentative, abusive, or inept.[10] Sometimes, a customer's only offense is belonging to some demographic group or nationality that is thought to be rude, argumentative, abusive, or inept. Many employees simply avoid these customers, providing minimal service. Others, however, get even, for example, by ridiculing these customers with patronizing comments when customers ask irritating and stupid questions.

Our favorite example of company employees taking revenge on customers comes from Regina Barreca's book, *Sweet Revenge*.[11] After a flight is canceled, an angry passenger waits in a long line to get rebooked onto a different flight. When his turn finally arrives in front of the ticket agent, Sonya, he launches into a tirade, abusing her about how incompetent she and her employer are; all the while Sonya is going out of her way to help him. Sonya recounted, "His last words were 'If everybody working for this organization is as incompetent as you, no wonder your airline loses money.' He then stormed off. I wished him a good flight as if nothing had happened.

"The little old lady behind him in line had heard everything, of course, and she sweetly asked how I managed to stay so polite and cheerful in the face of his abusive behavior. I told her the truth. 'He's going to Kansas City,' I explained, 'and his bags are going to Tokyo.' "

Litigation

Earlier, we discussed the story of Justin Callaway and his crusade against Cingular/AT&T. He filed a class action lawsuit to teach the company a lesson. In our research we found that for some avengers, going through the legal system is one way to get even. But it was not a frequently chosen course of action.

To gain some insight about situations where people do pursue the litigation route, consider the story of Jack, a middle manager at a global defense company. Jack had been a prized employee, moving up the managerial ranks quickly. That is, until a new project manager came onto the scene. This new manager and Jack did not get along with each other from the beginning. Despite Jack's best efforts and high performance rating, the project manager began to bad-mouth Jack's performance. In Jack's eyes, he was the target of slanderous comments. When he was later let go for so-called performance reasons, he decided to get even. Jack felt that litigation was the "only means available for me to get justice publicly. Just filing the lawsuit made the papers." Jack and the company settled the lawsuit out of court. For some people, then, this kind of public accusation against a company or person satisfies the urge for revenge.

The Choices Avengers Make

Clearly, aggrieved employees who are contemplating revenge have choices. But which of the variety of ways open to them do they choose, and when—and why? In short, two factors influence what would-be avengers choose: their personalities, and the amount of power they feel in the situations and organizations in which they find themselves. Personality is a factor because not all employees react the same way to the same situation: some are inherently more vengeful than others. Power is a factor (and a bigger factor) because it emboldens victims to act. Beyond these factors, avengers may contemplate a number of tactical considerations. Our list is not exhaustive, but it represents strategies our respondents have confessed using and that we have observed in our own workplaces.

The Personality Factor

We all know that people are different. Even in the same situation, different people often act differently. In workplace conflicts, some employees are more easily offended than others, some are quicker to perceive sinister motives behind offenses, some anger more easily, and some express their anger in a more aggressive manner. In short, some employees are just more volatile and vindictive than others.

Can anyone predict which employees are which? Yes, to some degree. Although in most of our own interview-based research we do not know what our subjects' personalities were, in our survey-based research we sometimes had respondents complete personality tests, so we could measure which traits correlated with more vengeful responses. Also, in other research on workplace conflict, and on aggression in general, scholars have given personality tests while measuring how much conflict people engaged in. Across many of these studies, some of the same personality traits keep coming up as predictive of revenge or aggression. Here is the list (so far):

- Gender: Men more than women[12]
- Chronically angry people[13]
- "Negative affectivity"—that is, people high in this trait tend to have negative moods, be distressed, nervous, and pessimistic, and are sensitive to negative events[14]
- "Unstable self-esteem"—that is, people who have high opinions of themselves, but these opinions are fragile and easily threatened[15]
- "Hostile attribution style"—that is, people high in this trait tend to see malicious and hostile intentions behind benign acts[16]
- Believers in the norm of reciprocity—that is, that every good deed should be rewarded and, especially, every bad deed punished[17]

To better remember this list, or at least what the common underlying trait is, listen to the wisdom of "Mary" from one of our studies. Mary told us that she was wary of the "collectors of injustices" in her workplace. She observed that, in her experience, such people sought revenge more often.

Our personal experience is consistent with Mary's—and with the research. We also know people who collect injustices, and they do seem more enthusiastic about revenge—and they tend to share many of the traits we have just listed. For instance, collectors of injustices look for (and find—and remember) slights in others' ambiguous comments. Thus, if collectors of injustices frequently find and remember slights, they may be insecure about their status, thus having inflated and unstable self-esteem. Also, if collectors of injustice find such slights in others' *ambiguous* comments, they may be making hostile attributions, and thus they may be higher in the trait of the hostile attribution bias. And why might that be? Maybe collectors of injustice also have a pessimistic worldview, fear the worst of people, and become irritable. That is, maybe they are high in negative affectivity. Also, if collectors of injustices believe in the norm of reciprocity—that is, that every good deed should be rewarded and every bad deed punished—then they may feel more justified in retaliating for the slights they perceive. Finally, if they are chronically angry, it may take only a little justification for them to strike back. Also, some evidence shows that anger over one incident may affect appraisals of ambiguous future incidents. That is, angry people (at least chronically angry people) go out looking for events that will make them angry, and thus have a tendency to perceive ambiguous incidents as unjust and to blame others rather than themselves.[18]

Now, we can hear the managers out there who are reading this saying, "Great! Where do I find tests for these traits that I can add to the battery of tests we give to applicants for jobs at my company?" Well, don't get too excited. Here's the bad news: although these traits can predict who at work is more likely to seek revenge, they don't seem to explain more than about 10 percent of the variance. That is, of all the revenge acts that occur, cumulatively these traits are responsible for less than 10 percent of them, roughly speaking. In only one study of which we are aware, by Scott Douglas and Mark Martinko, did these personality traits explain significantly more—about 62 percent of the variance of self-reported workplace aggression among transportation workers and public-school system employees.[19]

All this means that even though these personality traits can predict revenge, they don't predict it very accurately. That is, for nearly every person who might score high on these traits and who really will seek revenge at the slightest provocation, there's another person who scores high on these traits who isn't easily provoked, and someone who scores low who is easily provoked.

So what's a better predictor of vengeful behavior? The situation. Specifically, how much power the victim has and how fair the organizational procedures are.

The Power Factor

A very important feature of the situation in which revenge might occur is how much power the victim has. In particular, what position does the victim hold in the organization chart? Is the victim high in the chart, in upper management, perhaps a vice president or even the CEO? Or is the victim low in the chart, perhaps a first-line supervisor? There are many other ways to think about power besides where one sits in the organizational hierarchy—most textbooks in leadership and organization behavior, for instance, define *power* at least a half-dozen ways. But in our surveys of workplace revenge with our colleague Karl Aquino, we measured power as the victim's place in the organizational chart, and we found that this measure of power repeatedly predicted revenge. To be precise, we found that a victim's place in the hierarchy affects revenge in two ways.[20]

First, the higher placed a victim is in the hierarchy, the *less* likely the victim is to get even—at least in organizations where most employees don't act aggressively.[21] Why? One possible reason is that highly placed employees are more visible employees. That is, the higher you rise in an organization, the more other employees pay attention to what you do. Think about it: how many employees and other organizational constituents (for example, shareholders, customers) know who the CEO is, or even a division head, and care what that person does? All employees and major shareholders know; so do at least a few customers. Compare that level of attention to that focused on, say, a first-line supervisor, someone who is among scores of first-line supervisors spread across dozens of units, to whom only a handful of employees report. How many employees know who that first-line supervisor is and care about what that supervisor does? Not many. So higher-placed employees receive more attention, and because they receive more attention, they have to be more cautious about engaging in activities that others may deem unbecoming of a company officer—such as revenge. In short, higher-placed employees are less likely to get even, perhaps because they fear getting caught would undermine their credibility, and thus ultimately, their power.

Karl Aquino has suggested another possible reason: it may be that lower-placed employees are easier to offend. In some ways, low-placed employees may have something in common with gang members: because, compared to other members of society, they have fewer affirmations of social status—such as prestigious titles, high salaries, important assignments, and large reputations—they are more insecure about their status, which may leave them with unstable self-esteem and thus more easily threatened by slights.[22] If so, then low-placed employees may (over) react more to the same triggers—and perhaps especially by direct attacks on their reputations (whether "yo mama is so . . . " or "your quarterly report is riddled with inaccuracies")—than would higher-placed employees.

We found a second way that a victim's place in the hierarchy affects revenge. When victims are *more* highly placed *than the offender*, then victims are *more* likely to get even.[23] For instance, a middle-level manager is more likely to get even with a peer or a subordinate than with an upper-level manager. Why? Simply, employees who are offended by their supervisors are afraid to get even. Specifically, these offended employees fear losing opportunities and perks their bosses can provide, and offended employees fear triggering counterretaliation from their more powerful bosses. In so doing, they adhere to the adage Chris Matthews presents in *Hardball:* "Don't get mad; don't get even; get ahead." Political expediency can be a powerful motive that may override other motives to get even.

Beyond personality and status, some other factors help determine how victims evaluate their power and decide whether to act on it. These factors include the fairness of the organization's procedures and the tactical considerations of the immediate situation.

Fair Procedures. We mentioned in Chapter Three that fair procedures are important because procedural injustice can be an offense that triggers revenge. However, procedural justice is important for an additional reason: once someone is offended, whatever the trigger, the presence of fair procedures can direct the desire for revenge into official grievance channels instead of into idle, vigilante hands. When employees perceive that the organization uses fair procedures—that is, applies rules consistently to everyone, gives employees input into decisions that affect them, makes sure information going into decisions is accurate and truthful, suppresses conflicts of interest, and allows appeals—then employees are more willing to turn over their disputes to organizational authorities rather than pursue vigilante justice themselves. When procedures are fair, victims more likely believe they will get a fair hearing, and that offenders will get their due. In other words, employees who believe the organization will punish an offender are willing to let the organization do the dirty work itself and deal with the offender. Conversely, if employees instead believe the organization won't do anything about an offense, then justice can be achieved, they think, *only* if they take things into their own hands. So, employees who want justice—and most victims want justice—may find some way to punish the offenders themselves.

So how do fair procedures affect the use of power? In our studies, we find that it's not so much power alone, nor procedural injustice alone, that predict revenge. Rather, it's the combination of power and injustice that predicts revenge. Specifically, *only when* employees occupy a lower rung on the organizational ladder than their offenders, *and* employees perceive fair procedures, *then* employees are inhibited from seeking revenge.[24] To be clear, fair procedures alone won't inhibit revenge, nor will occupying a lower rung than one's offender alone inhibit revenge; it has to be the combination.

It would appear from these results that most victimized employees are would-be vigilantes. That is, first, when victims have power over their offenders, the victims are more likely to choose revenge, whether they think the organization might fairly punish the offenders or not. Second, when victims believe the organization will not fairly punish the offenders, the victims are more likely to choose revenge. In the first case, it may be that highly placed victims find it more expedient to punish offenders themselves than deal with the hassle of turning the dispute over to higher-ups. In the second case, because organizational authorities won't punish offenders, perhaps victims, even low-power victims, will risk counterretaliation in the search for justice. In short, the default is to consider revenge, but the special combination of power and fairness overrides that default.

At least, that's what we find in our surveys so far. We should clarify here that the "default to consider revenge" is not that strong a default. That is, we find that the combination of low power and high fairness make the revenge act, which is already somewhat unlikely, *very* unlikely.

Tactical Considerations. The results we've seen suggest that victims may choose how to get even based, in part, on tactical considerations of what is likely to be effective and efficient. Some tactical considerations we have noticed include multiplicity, forming coalitions, timing, and disguise.

- *Multiplicity.* When individuals get revenge, it often is not just a single act of revenge. Sometimes individuals may repeat the same act over and over. For example, upon having one's status degraded, the victim may have to lob many insults to degrade the status of the offender. That is, why lob one insult when many will do?

  Other times individuals may use a variety of revenge acts. For revenge to be successful, it may require a variety of acts, much as an effective political strategy often requires many activities—reward a colleague to recruit an ally; coerce another colleague into not being an ally of the adversary; befriend another colleague to collect information; promote one's own successes; demote the successes of one's adversary; get control of meeting agendas, and so on. For example, to get even with a coworker, an employee may bad-mouth the coworker to other coworkers; document the coworker's mistakes; freeze out the coworker; tattle by reporting the coworker's mistakes to the boss—and when the boss does nothing, do an end run around the boss by reporting the mistakes to the boss's boss. These multiple acts of revenge form a clear pattern that suggests a defamation strategy.

- *Coalitions.* Sometimes revenge is the work of one person acting alone, and this is usually the case in the violent episodes of revenge that are reported in the news. Other times revenge is an act committed by several people, such as in corporate "bitch sessions" where employees get even with a perpetrator by sharing stories. Earlier, we reported the example where the several employees who hated their boss got together and performed a voodoo ritual. In general, many indirect methods of revenge require the assistance of others.

• *Timing*. Just as in other conflicts, sports and otherwise, timing can be a critical element to revenge strategies. For example, if the goal of an avenger is to "teach a lesson" to the offender, then the lesson is only learned if the offender connects the avenger's revenge to the offender's provocation. In the absence of direct, candid communication ("This is about getting even with you for the time you..."), such connection depends on timing. For example, the longer the revenge occurs after the provocation, the more likely the offender will mistakenly connect the revenge to some intervening event or not connect it at all. Also, if the context or object of revenge resembles or "matches" the context or object of the provocation, then a tighter connection is made. A good match occurs, for example, when an avenger takes an "eye for an eye." A poor match occurs if the avenger takes an arm for an eye.*

• *Disguise*. Sometimes, however, avengers time their revenge not to make sure the offender gets the lesson, but instead to *disguise* their identities to make sure they do not get caught, for at least two reasons. First, many avengers fear counterretaliation by the offender, especially in the cases of powerful, tyrannical bosses. We analyzed episodes of workplace tyranny and discovered that, to cope with tyranny, employees are two-faced: they have a public and a private face.[25] Of particular interest here are the politics of disguise, where publicly employees agree with the boss, but privately they disagree and often dislike the boss. Second, many avengers fear the judgment of observers who may view the revenge act as immature, petty, immoral, or otherwise inappropriate. Thus, avengers with these fears would prefer *delaying* their revenge

---

*Matching matters not only in terms of helping the offender connect the revenge to the provocation, but also matters in justifying the revenge. Justified revenge is proportional—that is, the punishment fits the crime. More on this aspect in Chapter Eight.

so that nobody connects the revenge to the offense, thereby realizing who the avenger is. In short, avengers use timing to protect themselves.

Another timing issue involves having access to *available resources,* including the offender's time schedule and other personal information, and ensuring that the offender will be at the right place at the right time. If, for example, revenge requires props, then those props must be on hand. If a defamation strategy requires access to a meeting where the perpetrator's achievements or character will be discussed, then the avenger must be there and the topic needs to be on the agenda.

Now that it's clear what triggers revenge and what inhibits revenge, what can and should managers do? For that answer, turn to Chapter Seven.

7

PREVENTING REVENGE BEFORE IT HAPPENS

Practical Advice for Managers— And Would-Be Avengers

> It is folly to punish your neighbor by fire
> when you live next door.
>
> *—Publilius Syrus*

As the quote that opens the chapter (from the first century B.C.E., no less) illustrates, revenge can be a dangerous activity. And as shown in the examples throughout this book, revenge is often distracting and destructive to working relationships. It's not always bad—sometimes revenge results from relatively benign motives and the consequences can be positive for most stakeholders—but that appears to be more the exception than the rule. And even when revenge produces more good than harm, it's still not something that managers really want, if for no other reason than that it's chaotic, risky, and a sign of other problems. So how to prevent it?

Based on our model of how and why revenge happens, you have a good understanding about how to *predict* revenge. Our advice on how managers and organizations can help *prevent* revenge from occurring follows from our model. For instance, once you know what triggers revenge, you can focus on removing triggers from the workplace, where possible. Where that's not possible, then you can focus on shaping victims' blaming activities by helping them reduce the number of mental tricks they play on themselves. For those victims who harbor a desire for revenge anyway, which makes them would-be avengers, you can work on channeling their anger into official grievance mechanisms instead of into acts of revenge—or as discussed in Chapter Eight, even on channeling their anger into forgiveness.

But in this chapter we also offer advice to would-be avengers themselves—in the form of ten questions that we call "Counting to Ten" that anyone contemplating revenge should consider before acting. These are questions that managers will also find helpful for talking down a disgruntled employee. We begin with some specific ideas that managers and organizations as a whole can use to prevent revenge from occurring in the workplace—and dealing with it if it has already happened.

Practical Advice for Managers: No Justice, No Peace

Suppose you are a manager who wants to prevent your employees from seeking revenge against each other, or against you, or against the company. What can you do? The answer comes down not to picking better employees—which is not an option for many managers even if it were an answer—but rather to treating your current employees better. Even the best employees, treated badly, may still try to get even with each other and with you. So we offer two key pieces of advice:

- Don't provoke employees yourself.
- Be ready with a constructive response when employees provoke one another.

Don't Provoke Employees Yourself

Starting with the beginning of our model as outlined in Chapter Two (an offense occurs), the obvious advice is don't trigger your employees' wrath; don't be the offender. This means don't disrespect them, especially in public, and keep your promises and follow the rules. It also means not only refraining from unfair managerial practices but also going out of your way to make sure that employees *perceive* that your fair managerial practices are in fact fair.[1] Otherwise, even when you are fair, your employees—not knowing what you know—may still perceive you as unfair.

For instance, occasionally you have to deny requests. You may have to tell one employee who asked for a promotion that the promotion went to another employee, or tell the members of one unit that their budget proposal was turned down while another unit's was accepted. When this happens, employees whose requests you denied may perceive that you are obstructing their goals or treating them inequitably. Turning down employees and having them get upset about it is, of course, unavoidable and goes with the territory of being a manager. Fortunately, much research shows that as long as employees perceive that the process is fair, they complain less forcefully about not getting the outcomes they wanted.[2] So be sure that when you make a decision, your employees know the following about how you made it:

- *Rules were applied consistently.* The rules didn't change suddenly, and the same rules applied to everybody—that is, no one was above the law.
- *Employees had a voice.* You did not make decisions about their fate without at least consulting them.
- *Information was accurate.* All information feeding the decision was fact-checked, and if not all facts were unbiased, then at least other balancing perspectives were sought.
- *There were no conflicts of interest.* You personally had little to gain from the way the decision turned out. Or, if you did have something to gain, then you recused yourself as much as logically possible.
- *The decision is correctable.* The decision can still be changed or corrected, if necessary, through your reconsideration or through some kind of official appeal process.

Ideally, your decision-making process will be transparent enough so that these five features of process fairness will be obvious. But still you will likely need to remind employees over and over that these five features exist. Even so, be careful not to "protest too much" because many people interpret overly vigorous defenses as an indicator that something is being covered up.[3]

What to Do When Employees Provoke One Another

Just wishing that employees would stop fighting won't make them stop. Wishing that people would behave professionally and resolve a conflict themselves won't make them resolve it, though *sometimes* telling them to resolve it may work. No, as a manager you will sometimes have to get involved in their fights whether you want to or not. So, what role should you play in employee conflicts to help resolve them, or at least so that employees do not start getting even with each other? A manager can play three roles to decrease the odds that employees will get even: manager as first responder, manager as mediator, and manager as executioner.

Manager as First Responder. When one employee offends another, be the first on the scene. After all, you can't repair what you are not aware of. Therefore, employees need to believe that they can come to you with complaints—that is, that you are inherently fair and action-oriented and that you will address injustices. This is where using fair processes pays off a second time (the first time was in reducing triggers): when employees perceive fair processes, they perceive that management is more likely to punish offenders, and that motivates employees to come forward. So once an employee complains to you, you need to investigate that complaint—and investigate it promptly. If the complaint has merit, you act to restore justice.

Keep in mind that if you do not restore justice, then employees will consider restoring justice themselves. That is, you risk turning your employees into vigilantes. They may do nothing, particularly if they don't have the power to get away with revenge. Even so, they may hold on to resentment rather than forgive, and avoid the offender rather than work together productively. Restored justice is a better outcome. This is why encouraging employees to tattle on each other to you (presuming they tried to resolve their conflicts themselves first) can be worth the irritation of listening to tattling.

Manager as Mediator. If your organization has professionally trained mediators on staff, consider turning the dispute over to them. Trained mediators have better skills, and they are more likely to be perceived as neutral than you are, which encourages trust in the process, which should translate into the disputants' trusting each other more. Not all organizations, however, have their own professional mediators, especially not small organizations with limited resources. Although you could opt for hiring an outside professional mediator, it's also handy to have some informal mediation skills yourself, especially if you cannot afford or wait to find an outside mediator, or if doing so would make the conflict too formal and too awkward. You can hone your skills by reading any of a number of books on mediation, or even better, apply to join a neighborhood justice center in your community, which, if you are accepted, will train you as a mediator.

That said, we can recommend a couple of mediation actions to take yourself. Start by investigating the complaint. Because you use fair processes—and always remember Don Henley's three sides to a story ("yours, mine, and the cold hard truth")—you let the offenders tell their side of the story. After collecting all that information, you may reach either of two conclusions. First, the victim is mostly wrong, and there was no offense per se, just some circumstance the victim does not fully comprehend. Second, the victim is mostly right, and the offender really did offend the victim.

If you reach the first conclusion, then you should help the victim better understand the circumstances. Specifically, you can create doubts in the victim's mind about the offender's intentions. Remember, the perception of the offender having sinister intentions is critical to the victim's blaming the offender, and of course blame inflames the victim's desire for revenge. That is, it's not enough that there be a trigger; the victim must actually blame the offender, believing that the offense was done on purpose. Remember too that victims tend to play mental tricks on themselves that cause them to blame too harshly, and that's where you can interfere with the victim's blaming process.

Specifically, get the victim to reason through the offender's motives out loud. Then get the victim to doubt the certainty of those conclusions. How does the victim *know* the offender did it on purpose? For instance, is the victim overscrutinizing? Did the victim look for any evidence that would exonerate the offender? Has the victim talked to the offender or the offender's friends? Is there something the victim may have done to trigger the offender's offense? Generally speaking, here you are trying to talk the victim down from the edge of revenge. For other ideas on talking down victims, review the questions we list later in this chapter ("Counting to Ten"). One word of caution, though: to use this mediation tactic, you must be—and appear to be—neutral and trustworthy. Otherwise, this line of questioning could lead the victim to conclude that you are taking the offender's side.

If you reach the second conclusion—you decide the offender really did offend the victim—then encourage the offender to repent and apologize. Apologies go a long way toward restoring justice.[4] Or they do so with two exceptions: when the apology is insincere (the manager had to coerce the offender into apologizing, rather than the offender genuinely agreeing that it's the right thing to do); and when the harm done was motivated from a sinister intention rather than simple negligence.[5] Interestingly, one study found that apologies regarding negligence are even more successful if the offender makes an internal attribution in the apology (blames oneself rather than attributes it to circumstances), yet apologies regarding sinister intentions are more successful if instead the offender makes an external attribution (that is, blames the circumstances, as in "I had no choice; the situation forced my hand").[6]

Following an apology, the offender should make just amends.[7] If the offense was a goal obstruction, then the offender should give back whatever was taken, or offer something of equivalent value. If the offense damaged the victim's reputation, then the offender should help restore the victim's status. For instance, the offender could publicly "retract" any insult and then praise the victim. If the offense broke the rules or norms, then the offender should swear fealty to the rules, and give back whatever resource or advantage was obtained by breaking the rules.

Manager as Executioner. In the end, if the offender won't repent and apologize, or if the offense is so severe or of a type that means no apology would be sufficient, or if the offender has a history of offenses followed by empty apologies, then the manager should punish the offender. Moreover, because part of the purpose of punishing the offender is for the victim to perceive that justice has been served, the victim must know that punishment has been administered. (For what to do if revenge has already occurred, see the following box.)

What If You're Too Late?

Sometimes managers miss all opportunities to prevent acts of revenge from occurring. This happens especially when, as our data suggest, an avenger has more power relative to the offender; when the avenger is lower in the organizational hierarchy; or when the avenger perceives the workplace procedure climate as unfair. In these cases, the most important thing a manager can do is to prevent the offender from *counter*retaliating. Managers can advise offenders, for example, that rather than provoking the victim to further revenge, offenders should let the victim believe the score has been evened by not concealing how much the revenge act hurt. While "never let 'em know it hurt" may be good advice for dealing with bullies—because we don't want to reinforce bullies' aggressive behaviors with the reactions bullies seek—it's likely to be terrible advice for dealing with avengers, whose motives for harm are completely different. Justice-seeking avengers may keep coming back with more aggression until they believe they have evened the score—that is, until they *see* that they have caused as much harm as they felt from the original offense.

In organizations where confidentiality is of prime concern, however, victims often do not know what becomes of their complaints. Victims are rarely told if the offender was ever punished. While such secrecy may protect the offender from loss of face and protect the organization from defamation lawsuits by offenders, it does so at the increased risk of the victim's seeking further revenge against the offender. Again, the goal is to act so that employees perceive a procedurally fair workplace climate. If employees think that nothing happens to their complaints because they never hear of what results, then they may be less likely to complain next time and more likely to get even themselves.

We have seen exactly this problem in universities regarding complaints about student cheating. One student sees another student cheating and then officially complains by turning in the cheating student. The university then takes this complaint very seriously, and investigates whether the accused student cheated or not. But because these investigations are closed to the public to protect student reputations, the reporting student often never hears what happened to the student accused of cheating. Many such reporting students have concluded that, because they saw and heard no action, their universities took no action—and these students therefore are unlikely to bother reporting the next student they see cheating. The students' perception is wrong—but it's understandable.

What such universities need to do is follow up somehow without defaming individual students. For instance, a university could publish statistics, but not names, of the number of cases of cheating reported, the number of students convicted of cheating, and the types of penalties applied.

Counting to Ten: Ten Fateful Questions for the Would-Be Avenger

When angry count to ten before you speak.
If very angry, count to one hundred.

—Thomas Jefferson

Okay, so you've been harmed. Someone blocked your achievement of important goals, broke the rules, or assaulted your reputation in public. It looks like they did it on purpose. You feel not only angry but wronged, with righteous anger welling up inside you. What to do, what to do? Should you get even? If so, how?

Stop! Stop right there. Before you get even, take some time to more fully consider your situation. You don't want to do anything you will regret later. It's worth taking a moment to count to ten, or better yet, to ask yourself the following ten questions. Your answers could determine your fate and the fate of people around you.

1. Are you sure the offender deserves the retaliation?
2. Can the offender really be "taught a lesson"?
3. Will the punishment fit the crime?

4. Can you really get away with it?

5. Will you regret it?

6. Is it ethical?

7. Can you talk to the offender?

8. Can you talk to the boss?

9. Will no justice occur if you don't act?

10. Can you forgive the offender?

If you're a manager, you can use these same questions to talk down would-be avengers before they decide to take matters into their own hands.

1. Are you sure the offender deserves the retaliation?

To deserve your righteous retaliation, the offender must (at least) have *intentionally* harmed you. In that stunned moment when you first realize harm has been done to you, it's easy to assume that the harm was intentional. But was it? How do you know? Might you be playing mental tricks on yourself? Refer back to Chapter Four, and the mind game inside the blame game. Blaming correctly is important, because if you're wrong, and you treat the offense as if it were intentional when it was not, you're likely to launch a real conflict.

Our advice is to apply the maxim, *never attribute to malice what can be explained by stupidity*. To apply this maxim, revisit the various mental tricks that victims tend to play on themselves that make them believe the offender's harm was more intentional than it really was. Here's a short checklist:

• *Is it really about you?* Maybe it's about them. That is, maybe they weren't trying to harm you, but instead they just happened to harm you while engaging in some selfish pursuit of their own. Maybe they were trying to advance their career, and harming you just happened to help them toward that goal. While that is not a nice thing to do, it's still not as bad as picking on you because they dislike you, either. Or more benignly, maybe they just were negligent—they were not thinking about you at all, and harming you was an unforeseen side-effect of their plans. For instance, recall the point made earlier in the book—that your boss probably doesn't spend nearly as much time thinking about you as you do about your boss. Forgetting that finding, you might erroneously believe that your boss is thinking about you all the time, and that therefore everything your boss does to you must be intentional.

• *Are they really evil jerks?* Or are they just ordinary people reacting to an extraordinary situation? Keep in mind how the actor-observer bias may be distorting your thinking. That is, you are predisposed to perceive that others' harmful acts are due to their character flaws (whereas your harmful acts are due to unusual circumstances that pushed you to commit harm). But you may be wrong about that. And it's a good bet that they probably blame their circumstances. Certainly, they don't perceive themselves as evil jerks. If you treat them like evil jerks, then you cannot adopt their perspective. And if you cannot adopt their perspective, you cannot predict how they will react to your revenge. And if you cannot predict how they will react to your revenge, then revenge becomes a riskier act.

• *How strong is your evidence?* Would it stand up in court? You should consider the high standards of evidence that courts use, not because you might get sued one day but simply because they are good standards to use in organizational decision making. So how do you know what you think you know? Did the offender confess to harming you on purpose, or hating you, or even thinking about you much at all? Did a coworker hear such confessions straight from the offender's mouth and then tell you directly? Or, instead, did you hear only vague speculation at third- and fourth-hand? If so, then do you remember the old party game, "telephone," where one person whispers a story to a second person, who whispers it to a third, who whispers it to a fourth, and so on, until the last person in the whisper-chain retells the story to the group, and everybody laughs at how little it resembles the original, true story? Yeah, well, that's what's happening to you when you don't hear the offender's confession firsthand: you become the victim of telephone. If you cannot get firsthand information, then at least ask yourself how many coworkers support your conclusion. Do you have a representative sample of coworkers? That is, how many coworkers did you talk to? It needs to be more than a handful. Also, how did you pick the people you talked to? It's probably unrealistic for you to have picked them at random (which is what professional pollsters do), but at least you should have chosen some people from each camp in your office, including people who are friendly to the offender. Finally, did you ever search for evidence to prove yourself wrong about your initial suspicions that the offender is a jerk and did do it on purpose? Suppose you were wrong; what evidence would convince you of that? Look for that kind of evidence, too.

Go through this checklist *at least* two times before concluding that your offender deserves to be punished. Quite often—perhaps most of the time—you will find that the offender did not harm you intentionally: the offender was stupid, not malicious, and thus doesn't deserve punishment.

Also, as an insurance policy, create what our colleague Rod Kramer refers to as the "reality testing" system: a network of coworkers, confidants, and even family members who can act as a check and balance on your perceptions of any given situation. This network can offer invaluable input—especially when the stakes are so high.[8]

2. Can the offender really be "taught a lesson"?

A common motivation for workplace revenge is to teach a lesson to the offender.[9] Some possible lessons: "Do not harm me again." "Do not harm your employees or coworkers." "If you harm someone again, you will be punished, so it's in your best interest not to harm." "We have rules around here, and you *will* follow them."

But just because you *teach* the lesson does not mean that the person *learns* the lesson. (We're teachers—we know!) Why might the offender not learn? Here are several reasons:

- *The offender doesn't see the harm.* If the harm was accidental or negligent, the offender might not even be aware that you were harmed. Thus, for any revenge you implement, the offender will not connect it to having done anything to harm you, and so won't recognize your action as an act of revenge (unless you tell the offender, which, interestingly, many people don't seem to do). This means that the offender likely will, at best, be befuddled by your action, and, at worst, see it as the "first shot," a trigger to encourage the offender to seek (counter) revenge against you. This is how tit-for-tat feuds can start.

- *The offender believes you started it.* That is, the offender does recognize having caused you harm, but sees it not as unprovoked but as getting even with you for some harm that you caused first. The problem, then, may be that you don't remember what you did, or do not realize it hurt so much, and so you don't make the connection between what you did and what the offender did. Overall, the problem is that you're not keeping the same scorecard as the offender. You don't agree when the first round was, nor how many "points" a harm is worth. In all likelihood, the offender won't learn the lesson you had in mind. Instead, what the offender learns, if anything, is that you are the one who's a jerk.

- *The offender doesn't know that you are the avenger.* If your revenge must occur covertly—perhaps because the offender is much more powerful than you are, so you wisely fear counterretaliation—then the offender won't know (you hope) that you are the one who caused the harm. Because the offender doesn't know it was you, then the offender can't know what wrong the offender committed that has resulted in this painful outcome, and the revenge act will appear as a random act of unkindness from which there can be no lesson. (Unless the offender treats everybody in the office the same way, in which case knowing which employee did it is not necessary to make the connection.)

3. Will the punishment fit the crime?

Let's suppose the offender did harm you intentionally and really did start it, so you believe that punishing the offender is justified. OK, but how to punish, and how harshly should you punish?

If you were a court judge or jury, the answer would be relatively easy. Judges and juries can assign prison sentences or fines. Occasionally, however, judges get creative. For instance, a man was found guilty of posing as a U.S. Marine Corps hero from the Vietnam War. Technically speaking, he had served in the military, but he served in the army for two years, never saw combat duty, and did not earn any of the medals he wore to public events where he posed as a war hero. So U.S. District Court Magistrate Kelly Arnold sentenced the man to two years' probation and five hundred hours' service—service tending the graves of real Vietnam veterans! Here, most observers agreed that the punishment fit the crime. Also, note the importance of teaching a lesson, as reflected in U.S. prosecuting attorney Ron Friedman's comment to the press, "In this case, we thought it was a good idea to teach him what true service is like."[10]

What does *fit* mean exactly? We have always suspected that there is a certain artistic quality to revenge, something that transforms it from mere petty jealousy to poetic justice. As Arthur Lelyveld observed: "There is no denying the aesthetic satisfaction, the sense of poetic justice, that pleasures us when evil-doers get the comeuppance they deserve . . . . The satisfaction is heightened when it becomes possible to measure out punishment in exact proportion to the size and shape of the wrong that has been done."[11] (For more on what makes revenge "fitting," see the following box.)

The Artistic Qualities of Revenge

To better understand what makes revenge fitting—artistic and poetic rather than petty—we conducted a study with our colleague Karl Aquino in which we asked working professionals to imagine themselves as coworkers observing specific revenge scenarios.[12] We then had them judge the acts of revenge in terms of artistic merit and moral acceptability.

Here's what we found: First, when it comes to judging the consequences of a victim's revenge act, the amount of harm the victim-as-avenger causes the offender does not, by itself, determine observers' reactions. Instead, what observers care about is that the consequences of the revenge act are proportional to the harm caused by the offender's act. Revenge acts that are equal to their provocations in damage caused are judged as more acceptable, tolerable, just, and ethical than are unequal acts. The victim-as-avenger is also evaluated more favorably.

Interestingly, our data show that working people believe that too little revenge (underretaliating) is as unacceptable as is too much (overretaliating). This suggests that in the eyes of businesspeople, someone who is unwilling to inflict proportional harm upon an offender is seen in a negative light. All in all, these results show that a sense of proportion or symmetry is important.

This led us to predict that observers would judge more favorably revenge acts that used the same method to harm as the harm found in the trigger: what one early researcher called essentially a "photographic copy of the original crime in reverse."[13] For instance, if the offender insults the victim, and the victim then insults the offender back, that's the same method, and should, we thought, be viewed more favorably; whereas, if the victim instead froze out the offender, that would be a dissimilar method, and be viewed less favorably.

But we found the opposite to be true. Why? We're not entirely sure, but the working professionals offered up some reasons. They noted that if the revenge act uses the exact same method as the initial harm, then the revenge lacks creativity. Perhaps worse, it also means that the revenge cannot be covert—after all, an offender who sees a photographic copy of the original harm can easily deduce that the agent must be the person who just received the same harm.

Consider Juan, a manager who was bad-mouthed by another manager, Jorge, when both were vying for the senior leadership position on a major project. Jorge got the position, and Juan blamed his loss on Jorge's bad-mouthing, To get even, he went to a company "blog" (intended as a place for employees to post concerns and complaints) and, writing under a pseudonym, started bad-mouthing Jorge. As Juan described it: "I attacked him viciously, slicing and dicing him. It felt so good. But my first mistake was to blog so soon after he got the promotion.... The next day he confronted me, but I said nothing. But he knew I did it. Now he has it out for me. It was so stupid of me to go so personal and so soon after he got the new position. But I was *so* angry."

An important element of punishment that fits is that it must be altruistic. That is, it's not enough for one's revenge act to help oneself; it's viewed more favorably if it benefits other employees. As one respondent in our research stated, "He was doing it for all of us, he was our bodyguard against a micromanaging boss. His actions were beautiful." By contrast, if an act of revenge is construed as motivated mostly by the self-interest of the avenger, then such egoism detracts from the artistic value of the revenge. As another respondent described a coworker: "He sought revenge only to improve his situation. He didn't give a damn about us, or the impact of his actions on us."

Similarly, David Danow analyzes revenge stories in classic fiction (such as *The Odyssey*). He observes that these stories contain an aspect of altruism, at least in that the avenger's acts serve a purpose larger than the avenger's own interests. Specifically, Danow refers to "heroic qualities" of avengers, where they act as "instruments of God's justice" who are not getting even just for themselves, but are seeking justice for all people and God.[14] Perhaps this underlies our fascination with comic book superheroes like Spiderman or characters like Inspector Harry Callahan in those Clint Eastwood *Dirty Harry* movies.

4. Can you really get away with it?

Okay, so you've gotten this far: you're sure the offender deserves it; you know you can teach the offender a lesson; and you can find a punishment that fits the crime. Even so, can you get away with it? Often, no.

You can get away with it only if at least two difficult conditions are met: your coworkers will approve, and the offender won't counterretaliate (at least not severely).

Social Approval. Will coworkers approve? If coworkers do not approve, then the costs of revenge increase. Rather than having coworkers who feel sorry for you, you may have coworkers who disrespect you and trust you less. But *should you care* what others think of you? Don't parents tend to advise children to not care too much about what others think of them? But while that can be good advice for children's self-esteem in playground politics, we think it's bad advice for managers' effectiveness in organizational politics.

As an employee, and especially as a manager, you need to care what others think of you. You need to be viewed as competent, benevolent, and having integrity[15]; you need to have people trust you as an honest and fair negotiator[16]; and you need to have your bosses trust you as a competent and loyal subordinate.[17] When people engage in revenge, they can look out-of-control instead of competent, or appear to be selfish instead of looking out for the interests of their coworkers or their bosses or the organization as a whole.

Consider the story of Jeannie, a young and up-and-coming manager in a consumer products company. Jeannie had received her MBA from a prestigious business school and had worked hard to get ahead. She had developed quite a winning record, and she was viewed as a clear star with a bright future. But when her company gave out new brand assignments, she got transferred to one of the less attractive positions. That night with friends at a bar, Jeannie drank too much and bad-mouthed some of her peers who got better assignments and the senior leadership team that had made the assignments. Things got so bad that the bar manager asked Jeannie's friends to take her home. The next day, Jeannie was the target of much gossip—and ridicule. She had lost a lot of political capital with her vengeful, drunken tirade against her peers and bosses.

So what makes people *approve* of revenge? First, as noted in the box, the punishment must fit the crime. It has to be altruistic, proportionate, and probably of different method. But it is not sufficient to inflict equivalent amounts of harm; all observers must also *perceive* equivalent amounts of harm. How? Somehow the avenger would have to draw attention to the magnitude of the trigger, and then work hard to match that magnitude in the revenge act. Also, the avenger should do something different to the offender from what the offender did to the avenger, or at least act covertly. If this advice sounds contradictory to you, it does to us too. That is, it seems difficult, if not impossible, to follow both pieces of advice simultaneously. Given that the avenger needs to do something qualitatively different—to play a different game—how can observers possibly conclude that a score has been evened across *different* games? Moreover, how does an avenger draw attention to the carefully calculated, equal magnitudes of harm while also operating covertly?

One thing we should tell you about our study on the artistic qualities of revenge (as described in the box) is that although proportionate consequences and dissimilar methods made observers approve revenge *more* than did disproportionate consequences and similar methods, the observers still did not approve of revenge very much. To be precise, on a 1–7 scale (where 1 = strongly disapprove, 4 = neither approve nor disapprove, and 7 = strongly approve) the highest average approval was about a 4.1. Perhaps all that symmetry considerations can do for an avenger is to attenuate the negative judgments of the avenger's coworkers—but not produce admiration. Social approval for revenge is tough to pull off.

Social approval for revenge is even tougher to pull off for employees who are highly placed in the organization, such as vice presidents. Too many employees watch and care about what senior leaders do, and it would very difficult to craft an act of revenge that every one of those watchers would approve.

Counterretaliation Risk. Whether you can get away with revenge or not depends on what the offender's likely reaction will be to your revenge. An offender who knows it's you who caused the harm may well retaliate. As detailed in Chapter Four, the offender probably won't perceive the conflict the same way you do, and thus will not see what you do as an act of revenge or as the act that evens the score. So the question becomes: What can your target do to you? If you're tempted to draw a bead on your boss, or someone who otherwise is an important organizational player on whom you depend to get your job done, remember that you may suffer a great deal of harm. Even if your target can't (or won't) fire you, you may wind up with unpleasant job assignments and a lousy performance appraisal, and get yelled at in the meantime. Our advice? Don't finish what you can't win. Don't start what you can't finish.

5. Will you regret it?

In one set of our interviews we focused on whether people, in hindsight, thought their act of revenge was generally good or generally bad.[18] Some regretted it, some didn't. Why? The reasons were different for each, but generally they focused on the consequences: when the revenge turned out as they predicted, they often improved their situations; however, others noted how unpredictable revenge is. People said revenge was good, and that they did not regret it, when they perceived, for example, that the revenge act helped others or themselves in some tangible way, corrected the perpetrator's behavior, or somehow was the only choice they had.

On the other hand, when people told us that their revenge was bad, and that they did regret it, the following reasons emerged:

- *It was unprofessional.* Many respondents who got even at work judged their own actions as "unprofessional." That word means a lot of different things to different people, much as does the equally vague and damning put-down "immature." Some people did define *unprofessional conduct* for us as power abuse and hypocrisy in that they were dropping to the level of their offenders. Even more respondents elaborated that getting even was an emotional act or decision, and therefore inappropriate. To them, professional behavior follows logical choices. And they regretted letting their emotions get the best of them.

- *It was too unpredictable*. Many respondents reported that getting even achieved outcomes they did not predict and did not want. Other respondents said that they could not predict the consequences, making getting even "too risky." One respondent reported that she spent more time worrying about what might happen as a result of her vengeful behavior than she spent enjoying evening the score. The moment of revenge can be intoxicating, but the long hang-over of waiting for and fearing a counterretaliation that never comes can be quite painful, as well as sobering.

- *It caused disproportionate harm*. In some cases, the consequences turned out to be more severe for the offenders than the avengers intended or could justify. For example, remember the incompetent and micromanaging supervisor from Chapter Two, who had three shift supervisors call him in on every minor emergency, day or night. Their goal was to make their supervisor weary of micromanagement so they could regain their autonomy. But their actions contributed to their supervisor's nervous breakdown, which ruined his career.

- *It hurt innocent bystanders*. In some cases, innocent bystanders were hurt in addition to or instead of the offenders. Some respondents reported hurting their coworkers, their accomplices, their departments, their organizations, or the families of offenders (such as when they got the offender fired).

- *It caused the offender to counterretaliate*. Upon feeling the sting of revenge, offenders became avengers themselves, sometimes counterretaliating, often by withdrawing support. When offenders controlled critical resources, the lack of support significantly hurt the avengers.

- *It left the problem unresolved.* Some respondents reported that getting even did not resolve the original problem; it did not correct or deter the offender's unwanted behavior.

Finally, if that list is too long to remember, then memorize Ambrose Bierce's concise warning: "Speak when you are angry, and you will make the best speech you will ever regret."

6. Is it ethical?

Okay, so you've gotten this far: you're sure the offender deserves it; you know you can teach the offender a lesson; you can find a punishment that fits the crime; you can get away with it; and you won't regret it. (Come on, did you really get this far?) But is it ethical?

There are *a lot* of ways to answer that question! You could turn to religion, for instance, as the world's major religions have tenets against revenge. You could turn to philosophy, but then which branch of philosophy: utilitarianism, social justice, human rights (to name a few major branches)? Many books are dedicated to these philosophies. So let us make just a couple of quick points here that are specific to revenge.

First, we've actually discussed social justice philosophy a lot already. Revenge can advance social justice only if the punishment fits the crime, but that takes care only of distributive justice (that is, the outcome is fair) but not procedural justice (that is, fair processes were used).

Second, if you are trying to achieve the utilitarian ideal of the greatest good for the greatest number, then you must take into account all the stakeholders and all the costs each stakeholder bears. The situation has three sets of stakeholders—the avenger, the offender, and the bystanders—and good outcomes and bad outcomes can happen to each (as we discussed already, in point 5).

Third, a factor many victims considered when judging the ethicality of revenge was the availability, or lack thereof, of other options. As Saul Alinsky persuasively pointed out, people feel morally justified in engaging in aggressive and morally question-able behavior when they perceive that there is no other option.[19] To drive home this point, Alinsky argued that the reason the dropping of the atomic bomb on Hiroshima and Nagasaki was so controversial is because of *when* the United States dropped it—that is, at the end of the war instead of at the beginning. In mid-1945, when the Allies' victory seemed inevitable, the United States had another option, which was to invade the main island of Japan (albeit a costly, bloody option). In early 1942, however, when much of the Pacific fleet was damaged in Pearl Harbor and Japan was winning battle after battle, had the United States had an atomic bomb then, there would have been no controversy about using it to bring an immediate end to the war. Few people would have seen any other option.

And indeed, often it may seem like there *are* no other options but revenge. That point of view reminds us of the quotation from the great U.S. Olympic ice skater Dan Jansen, who once said, "When you have exhausted all possibilities, remember this: you haven't." Indeed, there are *always* other options. You just may not like them very much. But they may not be as bad as you think. The remaining "Counting to 10" questions offer some options for the harmed employee to consider.

7. Can you talk to the offender?

We are amazed at the number of avengers who could have tried talking to their offenders, but didn't, before deciding to exact revenge. Why is it so hard to talk to someone who offends you? For one reason, many employees just don't like direct confrontations.[20] They find such conversations uncomfortable, especially in the "go along to get along" culture that pervades many offices. Another reason may be that victims don't trust the offender to respond honestly. Even so, there still is much information to be gleaned from an offender who is not completely candid. Finally, before you harm others, have the courage to face them, if for no other reason than to avoid what social psychologists call the "bombardier effect"—that is, it's easier to harm someone from afar than from up close, much as the wartime bombardiers in airplanes found it psychologically less difficult to kill a human from thirty thousand feet than did foot soldiers who often killed others from thirty feet or less.[21]

So start by meeting with your offender (for the use of e-mail, see box below). Say (politely, not accusingly) that you were offended. The offender may not know. As one executive said: "When I mentioned to her [her boss] that she had been so rude to me in a public meeting, she was stunned. She thought she had been a bit caustic, she was just challenging me to motivate me. I'm so glad I went to talk with her because I could have done something real bad to get even." As that story suggests, an offender who does know about the harm may incorrectly assume that it did not bother you that much. In our experience, most people, once they know how much something bothers you, won't do it again. Also, with most people you can find out whether the offender offended you on purpose. And then actively listen to what the offender says.

To E-mail or Not to E-mail ...?

This is *not* a question—at least when it comes to confronting an offender. Simply put: don't e-mail! A confrontation requires a sensitive, complete conversation that will, by most accounts, lead to a reconciliation. Yes, e-mail is tempting because we can perfectly compose what we want to say. But the tone of voice and interactivity that comes with face-to-face communication is usually more helpful. You can always plan what you want to say before approaching the person, anyway. If you do decide to use e-mail, then do it in the way this executive told us to do it: "I get my angry e-mail written, the one that could melt the earth, and I save it as a draft. Then I delete it the next day." This executive's habit is consistent with some recent research by Laurie Barclay and Dan Skarlicki, which shows that writing logs or journals where the victim reflects on the offense, writing down all the relevant thoughts and emotions, can make it easier to get over the offense.[22] Perhaps even more effective is for the victim to write about the offense from the likely perspective of the offender.[23] However you do it, just don't mix up those "draft" and "send" files! Log, don't blog!

If the person-to-person approach sounds like a lot of work and would be very uncomfortable, you're right—it is. Nonetheless, it usually beats the alternative of doing nothing or engaging in risky revenge. Such a conversation (and usually, reconciliation) ends the psychological costs of holding a grudge and the fear while waiting to see how someone responds to your revenge. What's more, reconciliation does not mean a lack of justice, as we discuss in more depth in Chapter Eight.

8. Can you talk to the boss?

If talking to the offender gets you nowhere—the offender refuses to talk, or will not apologize, or worse, offends you again—then go talk to the offender's boss or to an organizational authority assigned to employee conflicts (perhaps an ombudsperson, mediator, or union shop steward). That is, use official mechanisms to air your grievance. These outsiders have more power than you do, and often can force the offender to address your concerns. Note that many bosses prefer that employees attempt to resolve their own conflicts among themselves before involving the boss. We agree with the folk wisdom, "Bring your boss solutions, not problems." Show the boss that you tried to work out a solution among yourselves, but could not. If you don't show this first, your boss may lose some respect for you. If, however, the boss and organization have often not been fair, or if the boss is the offender, then this option may not work.

9. Will no justice occur if you don't act?

Must you seek revenge for justice to be served? Consider that justice might be served anyway even if you don't act. Often, others may see the offense and do something about it. Bosses may chastise offenders in private, but you hear nothing of it because it occurred behind closed doors (often because the boss does not want to cause loss of face to the offender).

Some of the people we interviewed discussed a belief in karma as a reason not to engage in revenge.[24] For some people, this was part of their religion, and to them it meant that offenders would have to account for their actions in the afterlife. For others, it was more a social phenomenon than a religious issue. They believed that—in this life—eventually everyone gets what's coming to them. Regarding offenders, one line of karmic reasoning goes like this: if an offender really has a problem, then that offender has offended others in the past and will offend others in the future. Eventually, this repeat offender will cross the wrong victim—a victim who will seek a horrible revenge against the offender. In the meantime, the repeat offender may be sabotaging relationships in the workplace, getting less of the cooperation and resources needed to do well. Perhaps that is justice. Or at least justice enough to make it not worth your while to spend mental, social, and political resources just to add an incremental level of justice.

10. Can you forgive the offender?

That is, can you let go of the resentment and the anger? As Mike McCullough has spent the last decade investigating, this is a real option that many victims choose and one well worth considering.[25] Consider forgiving the offender not so much for their benefit but for your benefit, for your own peace of mind. We have more to say about this option in the next chapter.

This chapter offers a lot of practical advice to managers and would-be avengers on dealing with revenge, with the goal of preventing it before it occurs. In the next chapter, we want to move beyond revenge and focus on forgiveness as an alternative response. Forgiveness is not easy, and for it to occur, some justice must be served beforehand—a process we call "the sequencing of virtues."

8

MOVING BEYOND REVENGE

Don't Get Mad, Don't Get Even— Get Ahead

To err is human, to forgive divine.

—*Alexander Pope*

A tale from the Cherokee goes like this: One evening, sitting by the fire, an old Cherokee told his grandson, "My son, the battle is between two 'wolves' inside us all. One is Evil. It is anger, envy, jealousy, sorrow, regret, greed, arrogance, self-pity, guilt, resentment, inferiority, lies, false pride, superiority, and ego. The other is Good. It is joy, peace, love, hope, serenity, humility, kindness, benevolence, empathy, generosity, truth, compassion, and faith."

The grandson thought about it for a minute and then asked his grandfather: "Which wolf wins?" The old Cherokee replied simply, "The one you feed."

Throughout this book, we have been focusing on a very human response: revenge. No one likes to talk about revenge in public, but as everyone knows, revenge is part of the social fabric of everyday life—and this is why revenge fascinates everyone and captures the imagination.

But, as in the Cherokee tale, life offers an alternative to choosing the negative emotions and thoughts that feed the desire for revenge. And that alternative is forgiveness. Now, most people have heard the saying, "To err is human, to forgive is divine," which is a slight variation of the actual quotation from Alexander Pope. But forgiving an offense is a hard thing to do (we know this is true for the two of us), particularly when we have been wronged or harmed unfairly.

Even so, perhaps forgiveness is the best way to go. Chris Matthews suggests as much in *Hardball*. "Don't get mad; don't get even; get ahead," he writes, and that seems like good advice to us. In this final chapter, we focus on forgiveness as one approach to getting ahead. When and why do people forgive others, and why do people find some offenses *unforgivable?* It turns out that the factors that encourage or discourage forgiveness are the flip side of the factors that motivate revenge.

Forgiveness in the Workplace

Forgiveness is the moral antithesis of revenge. Whereas a person who seeks revenge feels anger and resentment and wants to see the offender harmed, a person who forgives thereby becomes free of negative thoughts and emotions (rage, self-doubt, shame, humiliation) and consciously refrains from harming the offender, *even if the opportunity to do so presents itself.* When choosing forgiveness, the injured party deliberately forgoes retribution, punishment, and even a fair distribution of goods. It is for this reason that we define forgiveness as the forswearing of anger, resentment, and the desire to harm the offender.[1] In practice, this is often a lengthy process preceded by exercises in intellectual forgiveness (such as reflections and discussions with a third party that help the victim generate greater empathy toward the offender and recall instances of needing to be forgiven).

As negative thoughts and emotions toward the offender decrease through forgiveness, anxiety and depression decrease as well. Forgiveness also helps victims of harm regain a sense of self-worth and personal efficacy, both of which may have been threatened by the offense. And because forgiveness deflects attention from the offense, victims don't obsessively ruminate over past wrongs. For these reasons and others, recent research on forgiveness, such as that by Everett Worthington and his colleagues, demonstrates positive health effects of forgiveness. Forgiveness reduces the anger and associated physiological stress that can hurt health.[2] At the interpersonal level, forgiveness can help deescalate conflicts rooted in historical patterns of revenge and counterrevenge.[3] Why? Because when people exercise "merciful restraint" (that is, refusal to harm the offender) they break a pattern of negative reciprocity, thus providing an opportunity for rebuilding trust and cooperation.[4]

Why and when do employees choose forgiveness over revenge? As a human response to being harmed, forgiveness is not usually an easy choice. To discover the various reasons workers do and don't forgive, Bob interviewed employees from a variety of industries about their experiences with forgiveness.[5] What he found was revealing in terms of forgiveness and the unforgivable.

Four different categories of reasons emerged to explain why people forgive others in the workplace. One was when there was an *offering of truth* in which the offender provided a sincere acknowledgment of personal responsibility. A second was when there was an *offering of penance*, which took the form of an apology or compensation for the harm, or both. A third reason, *empathy*, occurred when the victim saw the offender as a flawed human being. Finally, a *conscious decision to regain control* was a fourth reason given when people saw their own anger as self-destructive.

The Offering of Truth

What victims are looking for first in the offering of truth is a sincere and honest explanation. And that explanation must be heartfelt and genuine. The explanation must acknowledge responsibility—and not just privately but also publicly.[6] Consider one manager, Briana, who forgave a fellow manager, Jim, who had taken credit for *her* ideas and parlayed that into a high-profile project assignment. "I was livid that he stole my ideas," Briana said. "I work my butt off every day, so when someone steals my ideas, it is payback time. I was ready to do so at a meeting with senior leadership, a meeting discussing the project that Jim was now leading.... As the meeting came to a close, senior leadership asked if there was anything else anyone wanted to add. I was about ready to say something when Jim began to speak.... Jim told people that the ideas were really mine, not his. There was complete silence in the room. I couldn't believe what I had just heard. Because Jim fessed up and told the truth, and did so publicly, I found it in my heart to forgive him. And I told him so."

The offering of truth may be one reason why doctors who give apologies for medical errors are sued for malpractice less often than doctors who refuse to give apologies (often out of fear that the apology will be perceived as an admission of guilt that may be used against them in court).[7] As Richard C. Boothman, chief risk officer for the University of Michigan, explained to the U.S. Senate, "People go to lawyers not because they want a million-dollar payout. People go to lawyers because they want answers and they don't trust their caregivers to give them answers. People go to lawyers because they don't get any information at all."[8] This is why many states have considered "I'm Sorry" laws that would give doctors legal immunity for admitting mistakes.[9] The intent is to help improve communication between doctors and their patients and avoid conflict escalation.

Improving communication and truth-telling work not just at an individual level but also at a nation-state level. As we know, the demand for truth was a critical element for political transition and a people moving forward in a post-apartheid world of South Africa. The Truth and Reconciliation Commission was created to link truth with reconciliation, if not forgiveness. Although the Truth and Reconciliation Commission has not been hailed by all as a complete success, many people have credited it as being essential to the peaceful transition of power in post-apartheid South Africa.[10]

The Offering of Penance

When offenders offer some form of penance for their wrongdoing, people are more willing to forgive them. Consider the story of Doug, an office manager at a food company. Doug had gone ballistic when his boss forced him to work overtime and miss his son's championship swim meet. Doug was so angry that he considered quitting. But before he could quit, his boss apologized. In Doug's own words: "After hearing that I was so upset because I missed my son's swim meet, my boss came to me and apologized," Doug recounted. "He was truly sorry. He said he didn't fully appreciate the impact of his decision on me and my son. I accepted his apology and I forgave him."

But an apology isn't the only form of penance that can lead to forgiveness. Attempts to restore the loss or harm can motivate forgiveness. Consider the story of Jerry, a production worker in a manufacturing plant. Jerry had been fighting with Frank, another production worker. The fight was over the trashing of Jerry's locker by Frank and his buddies as part of a prank. Unfortunately, the prank got out of hand and some very special photographs of Jerry and his deceased mother were torn in half. Jerry was furious with Frank and confronted him about the photos, throwing them in Frank's face. Frank just laughed it off. Frank learned soon after of the significance of the photos to Jerry and arranged for the photos to be restored by a professional. When Frank gave the restored photos to Jerry, Jerry was overwhelmed. In Jerry's words: "When I saw the restored photos, they looked new. I almost cried. I didn't cry, but I forgave Frank. I offered him my hand and we shook."

Empathic Response

Another factor motivating forgiveness was empathy. When the victim could see the offender as a human being, someone with human failings and limitations, then forgiveness was possible.

The ability to humanize his abusive boss was what led one employee, Rick, to forgive him for how he treated Rick and his team. As Rick put it: "Day in and day out, my boss would attack me and my team publicly," he said. "So I went to see him to demand a change in his behavior. As I arrived at his office, I saw him on the phone, crying. As I listened to him talk, it was clear his wife had left him and taken the children. I felt for him, and I decided at that point that, even though he had been a jerk to me and my team, he was still a human being, imperfect like us all. I just had to forgive him."

Conscious Decision to Regain Control

When people have been victimized, their desire for revenge grows, as illustrated in the stories and examples throughout this book. Sometimes those emotions can exercise a stranglehold, as described in Chapter Five. But, occasionally, with the help of family, friends, or even a therapist, people come to realize that the feelings of revenge have taken over their lives—and not for the better. With that new awareness, people can make a conscious decision to regain control over their lives through the act of forgiveness. Or, in the words of a senior manager in a federal agency: "With the help of my wife and my pastor, I lifted the burden of my anger off my shoulders, a weight I had carried for two years. I forgave my superior for his abusive behavior. I was now in control of me."

These results are consistent with other research on the motivations to forgive among workers.[11] For instance, David Bright and his colleagues, who interviewed workers in a unionized trucking company, also found that victims sometimes offered forgiveness "pragmatically"—that is to say, they saw it as in their best interests to forgive their offenders.[12] But Bright's group also found another reason, "transcendence," where victims wanted to learn from the experience and focus on positive thoughts and emotions as a learning experience. For victims, it was the principle of the thing. A recent survey of workers by Fox and

Bennett also found similar motives: a self-interest reason, a principle-based reason (that is, some people just believe in forgiveness as a moral or religious principle that they must always follow), and a penance-based reason where some workers forgave in return for receiving penance and apologies.[13]

Finally, our results are also consistent with the forgiveness research in non-work contexts. Summarizing this research in his book, *Beyond Revenge: The Evolution of the Forgiveness Instinct*, psychologist Michael McCullough recommends three actions the offender should take to promote forgiveness: apologize, while accepting responsibility (though see the discussion in Chapter Seven about when and how to accept responsibility); make self-abasing gestures to show that one is truly sorry, such as showing shame, guilt, and embarrassment, which increase the perception of the sincerity of the apology; and compensate the victim at least a little (it does not have to be full compensation to encourage forgiveness).[14]

Why and When Do Workers *Not* Forgive?

But not all harms or offenses are forgivable. Bob found three different categories of reasons why people decided not to forgive others in the workplace. First was the category of *shattered assumptions*, which meant a betrayal of private confidential material or the betrayal of a trusted relationship. The second category was *damaged identity*, which meant an unfair characterization of the person or the person's work, or that the person felt wrongly accused, or was the target of insults around gender, race, or religion. The final category was labeled *interpersonal indignities*, which referred to people being lied to or deceived, or feeling used or manipulated for another's gain.

Shattered Assumptions

Can there be anything as powerful, in terms of its emotional fallout, as when one is betrayed by another? In the workplace, betrayal is a cardinal sin in the eyes of many—and it is often an unforgivable offense. Even in the consumer context, research shows that when firms give poor service to their best customers, those customers actually feel betrayed, and they rarely come back for more business.[15] In our data, whether it was a betrayal of confidence or a betrayal of a trusted relationship, the offender responsible for the betrayal found that no amends could correct the situation. The psychological experience of betrayal was described by victims as "shattered assumptions." What they had thought to be true, what they thought to be an ordered world where others looked out for their interests, was no longer true or ordered, if ever. In the words of an educational consultant: "I had trusted my colleague with some very private details about my personal life," he said. "I swore him to secrecy. I found out that two weeks later he told a couple of senior partners my secrets. I was devastated. How could he have done that to me? Our friendship wasn't just fractured, it was shattered . . . . I will never forgive him."

Damaged Identity

As discussed in Chapters Three and Five, a damaged identity or reputation is a powerful trigger of revenge, one that can generate the hottest of emotional responses. Whether it is an unfair characterization of someone's character and work, or a wrongful accusation, or an insult, the damage done to reputation or identity can prove irreparable. It can also be unforgivable, as Michael, a senior project manager in an information products company, described the behavior of his boss, Jeffrey. In Michael's words: "It was a stupid, narcissistic decision to replace me. The only way he could justify it was to tear me down in public, saying I was incompetent even though I had several consecutive successful years as the project head. He couldn't admit he had screwed up—the new head was driving the project into the ground. So he attacked me and my integrity. I will never forgive him."

Interpersonal Indignities

Interpersonal indignities were among the key triggers of revenge—often creating intense and lingering feelings of anger. The examples of being lied to or feeling used by others strikes a deep emotional chord. Those who find such indignities unforgivable described their anger as grounded in "subhuman" treatment that violated their sense of human dignity. As Barbara, a middle manager in a small company that went bankrupt, described it: "They knew they were running us into the ground financially. But they deliberately hid it from us. Those lying bastards used us. There is a special place in hell for them. There is no atonement for their sins."

The unforgivable and the unforgiven make for strained working relationships and lingering conflict. Clearly, this is not what workers and managers want.

Toward Peace *and* Justice in the Workplace

What everyone wants in the workplace—from the lowest-level employee to the highest-level manager—is peace. Conflict is gut-wrenching, distracting, and usually unproductive. It clutters our minds with angry thoughts of comeuppances and dominating victories over our offenders. It often peppers our conversations with obsessive, disgruntled statements about our coworkers. It robs us of our sleep when we wake up in the middle of the night and start thinking about how we will deal with them. It grips us with a queasiness, if not fear, as we wait for the other party to respond to our revenge—will the offender accept it, or counterretaliate? How will it all turn out? Why is this taking so long?

Alternatively, perhaps we can have instant peace if only we could ignore the offense and reconcile with the offender. But peace at any price? Should we grant ourselves, our offenders, and all the bystanders peace if there is no justice? What is peace without justice? Peace without justice is tyranny, and it is ephemeral. Eventually, if injustice persists, some victims will seek revenge, even if many more victims resign themselves to their fates, or just plain resign from their jobs.

So, how can you have it both ways—peace *and* justice? Actually, our argument is that the only way to get peace or justice *is* to have it both ways: you cannot have real peace in the workplace without justice. Therefore, any movement toward peace, we argue, requires a sequencing of the virtues of forgiveness, reconciliation, and justice. Specifically, peace requires reconciliation; reconciliation is easier after forgiveness; and forgiveness occurs more easily after justice has been served.

Note that reconciliation is different from forgiveness. Reconciliation is a behavior, whereas forgiveness is a state of mind and heart. Reconciliation is an effort by the victim to extend *external* acts of goodwill toward the offender (for example, do favors, be friendly, cooperate) in the hope of restoring the relationship. Forgiveness is the *internal* act of relinquishing anger, resentment, and the desire to seek revenge against the offender. As Everett Worthington and his colleagues note, most forgiveness scholars agree on this point: "Forgiveness is not excusing, exonerating, justifying, condoning, pardoning, or reconciling."[16]

Because reconciliation and forgiveness are different, it is possible to have one without the other. For example, it is possible to forgive without reconciling: a victim can overcome negative emotions without hoping to, or even wanting to, restore a relationship with the offender. Sometimes people forgive and move on.[17] For instance, victims can recognize the humanity of the offender's flaws, but also choose not to expose themselves to those flaws again. Sometimes customers let go of their anger toward a firm, but they still do not purchase from that firm ever again. Conversely, it is possible to reconcile without forgiving: a victim may choose to cooperate with the offender even while still strongly feeling anger or resentment. This might occur if the victim finds it expedient or beneficial to maintain a relationship, when, for instance, the offender is the victim's boss. Alternatively, customers may continue to do business with a firm they now hate, because they have no choice (say, sticking with an airline because nobody else flies into your town, and you don't want to give up all those frequent flier miles).

Although reconciliation can occur without forgiveness, reconciliation is more likely if forgiveness occurs first. That is, it is easier to approach an offender, to offer an olive branch, after your negative emotions toward the offender have decreased. If the negative emotions toward an offender remain strong, however, it is more comfortable to avoid than to approach the offender, even if you have not opted for revenge. Therefore, in the workplace, whatever conditions promote forgiveness also make reconciliation more likely. The converse is not true, however: some conditions that promote reconciliation may not promote forgiveness. This is what we have found in our survey-based research with Karl Aquino. Reconciliation and forgiveness tend to go together, but not always.*

So, if forgiveness begets reconciliation, then what begets forgiveness? Scholars who study the aftermath of crimes note that victims more easily forgive their assailants if justice has first been served (that is, the assailant has been captured, prosecuted, and convicted).[18] In short, such forgiveness is *conditional* upon justice. Julie Exline and Everett Worthington, in particular, argue that the smaller the "injustice gap" (that is, the size of the difference between the magnitude of the original offense and the magnitude of the justice served) the easier it should be to forgive. The research on "restorative justice" makes a similar argument—once justice is restored after an offense, victims are likely to get over the offense and move beyond it.[19]

The point is clear: if we want peace in the workplace, we must have justice in the workplace. Justice leads to forgiveness, forgiveness leads to reconciliation, and reconciliation creates peace. It all begins with justice. And justice begins with leaders.

---

*That is, statistically speaking, they correlate strongly but nowhere near perfectly (in terms of statistics, in our study the Pearson r-value was .53, meaning that reconciliation explained about 28 percent of the variance in forgiveness).

A Call to Leadership

We presume that you picked up this book because you want to manage your employees in a way that will make them less likely to be vengeful in the workplace. Perhaps, as a leader, you feel it is your responsibility to promote peaceful productivity in your organization. When people are distracted with thoughts of getting even—when they are angry because their leaders and managers don't do anything to correct the injustices in the workplace—they can't bring their best to their job. It is up to you to answer the call of leadership that will not only bring peace but will also bring productivity. So, what should you do to answer this call?

Let's start with what you should *not* do. We hope we have dissuaded you from what appears to be many managers' first instinct: to find the "problem" employees who are most vengeful, and then keep a watchful eye on them. We also hope we have dissuaded many HR professionals from thinking the answer is finding the right personality test to avoid hiring such problem employees in the first place. The problem isn't so much the employees; the problem is the workplace, particularly an unjust workplace. Managers who try to fix the employee rather than the workplace are unlikely to find more than a temporary fix. Eventually, in a bad environment, many good employees will become bad employees.

Perhaps an analogy will help. Moe Maverick was the Tripp family beagle. And Moe was a *bad* dog. But he didn't start out that way. Moe was a purebred beagle—the dog had papers and everything—no puppy-mill puppy here. Also, Moe went to dog-training school, where he learned obedience and hunting skills. Unfortunately, after six months of being trained as a hunting dog, it was Moe's fate to become the pet of a family with six unruly children. And, oh, did those kids tease and abuse that dog. They would gang up on the dog, four at a time, standing in the four corners of the room, all summoning him at the same time. After their mom had freshly waxed the linoleum floors, they would put socks on the dog's paws, then place his dinner dish on the far side of the room, just around a tight corner, that the hungry and excited beagle would overshoot, sliding across the room into the far wall. Is it any wonder the dog developed a bad temperament? Moe Maverick, world's best beagle, was no match for the environment in which he found himself. That dog never did hunt.*

What should the Tripp family have done? Get a new dog? A better dog? What would be the point? Any dog with the misfortune to enter *that* household, no matter how well-bred and well-trained, would eventually have its training undone and its personality unhinged.

We think many managers view their difficulties with problem employees just this way. That is, they see their employees underperforming and misbehaving and wish their organization had hired better employees.[20] But all too often, newer, better employees would only work out temporarily; after a while, these employees too would begin to perceive and respond to their dysfunctional workplace climate, and eventually, they'd behave just like the other "problem" employees."[21]

Your job, then, is not to spot and control your vengeance-prone employees. That's ineffective; it's too hard to accurately predict which employees are more vengeful. Moreover, even if you could accurately spot the more vengeful employees, you would have to spend too much of your time monitoring them. There's also the danger that, by treating vengeful people as would-be criminals, they would perceive this treatment as unfair. And then your monitoring might backfire: in attempting to prevent revenge, you just might unleash it.

A more effective approach is to make sure you and your workplace treat employees fairly. By treating them fairly, not

---

*But Moe did get even with the Tripp family by doing well anyway, living for seventeen long years as a beloved (though mostly badly behaved) member of the family.

only do you avoid triggering revenge yourself, you also provide the sense of law and order that makes victims willing to turn over their grievances to the system rather than taking the law into their own hands. Remember, before they can forgive, victims expect some justice. If you do not provide the justice, they will be more likely to seek it themselves. When people undertake revenge, they gain a sense of justice, particularly if leaders and managers don't do anything to correct the injustice!

So do something. Specifically, to restore justice, as we argue in Chapter Seven, you need to first be aware of the offense, then investigate the offense, and then, if warranted, persuade the offender to sincerely apologize. If a sincere apology does not happen, then you may need to punish the offender—and make sure the victim knows the offender was punished. That way, the victim perceives that justice has been served, and the possibility for forgiveness emerges.

This is the final insight that we want to leave with you, as a manager and leader: some amount of justice is a precondition for forgiveness. And that is the call to leadership you must answer. It was the call to leadership answered in South Africa with the Truth and Reconciliation Commission. It was the call to leadership answered by Boston Archbishop Seán Patrick O'Malley, who went to victims of pedophile priests, listened to their pain, and acknowledged the truth of what happened. Archbishop O'Malley clearly heard the anger of the Archdiocese of Boston Catholics who were outraged at calls for forgiveness before any acknowledgment of the truth of what had happened, let alone any financial compensation for the victims.[22] And, following O'Malley's example, Pope Benedict XVI also met with victims of sexual abuse by pedophile priests in Washington, D.C., during his April 2008 trip to the United States.[23]

We hope that by reading this book you have gained greater insight into the psychological and emotional undercurrents of the soul of discontent in today's workplace. Certainly you will have a better idea of how to navigate the turbulent waters of righteous anger. But with this better understanding and new skills to deal with revenge comes a greater responsibility on the part of leaders. You must pay attention to the warning signs and triggers of revenge, and act accordingly; to do so goes to the core of virtue in leadership. Or as David Starr Jordan, the first president of Stanford University, so aptly put it:

> Wisdom is knowing what to do next.
> Skill is knowing how to do it.
> Virtue is doing it.

May this serve as a call to action to leaders and managers in the workplace everywhere.

Bibliography

Adams, J. S. (1965). Inequity in social exchange. In L. Berkowitz (Ed.), *Advances in experimental social psychology* (Vol. 2, pp. 267–299). New York: Academic Press.

Adams, J. S., & Freedman, S. (1976). Equity theory revisited: Comments and annotated bibliography. In L. Berkowitz (Ed.), *Advances in experimental social psychology* (Vol. 9, pp. 43–90). New York: Academic Press.

Alinsky, S. (1971). *Rules for radicals: A pragmatic primer for realistic radicals.* New York: Random House.

Allen, M. (2001, June 3). Bush aide details alleged Clinton staff vandalism. *Washington Post*, p. A01. Available online: www.papill-onsartpalace.com/trashing.htm. Access date: June 15, 2008.

Allred, K. G. (1999). Anger driven retaliation: Toward an understanding of impassioned conflict in organizations. In R. J. Bies, R. J. Lewicki, & B. H. Sheppard (Eds.), *Research on negotiations in organizations* (Vol. 7, pp. 27–58). Greenwich, CT: JAI Press.

al-Mugahbri, N. (2004, June 30). Tit-for-tat raid after fatal rocket attack. *Sydney Morning Herald.* Available online: www.smh.com.au/articles/2004/06/29/1088487964342.html?from = storylhs. Access date: June 18, 2008.

Anderson, C. A., & Bushman, B. J. (2002). Human aggression. *Annual Review of Psychology, 53,* 27–51.

Aquino, K., & Douglas, S. (2003). Identity threat and antisocial behavior in organizations: The moderating effects of individual differences, aggressive modeling, and hierarchical status. *Organizational Behavior and Human Decision Processes, 90,* 195–208.

Aquino, K., Douglas, S., & Martinko, M. J. (2003). Overt anger in response to victimization: Attributional style and organizational norms as moderators. *Journal of Occupational Health Psychology, 9,* 152–164.

Aquino, K., Tripp, T. M., & Bies, R. J. (2001). How employees respond to personal offense: The effects of blame attribution, victim status, and offender status on revenge and reconciliation in the workplace. *Journal of Applied Psychology, 86*, 52–59.

Aquino, K., Tripp, T. M., & Bies, R. J. (2006). Getting even or moving on? Status variables and procedural justice as predictors of revenge, forgiveness, and reconciliation in organizations. *Journal of Applied Psychology, 91*, 653–668.

Asch, S. (1951). Effects of group pressure upon the modification and distortion of judgment. In H. Guetzkow (Ed.), *Groups, leadership, and men* (pp. 177–190). Pittsburgh: Carnegie.

Axelrod, R. (1984). *The evolution of cooperation.* New York: Basic Books.

Axelrod, R. (1997). *The complexity of cooperation: Agent-based models of competition and collaboration.* Princeton, NJ: Princeton University Press.

Banaji, M. R., Bazerman, M. H., & Chugh, D. (2003). How (un)ethical are you? *Harvard Business Review, 81*, 56–64.

Barclay, L. J., & Skarlicki, D. P. (in press). Healing the wounds of organizational injustice: Examining the benefits of expressive writing. *Journal of Applied Psychology.*

Barclay, L. J., Skarlicki, D. P., & Pugh, S. D. (2005). Exploring the role of emotions in injustice perceptions and retaliation. *Journal of Applied Psychology, 90*, 629–643.

Barreca, R. (1995). *Sweet revenge: The wicked delights of getting even.* New York: Harmony Books.

Barsella, R. M. (2007, July 2). Sincere apologies are priceless. Nurse.com. Available online: www.sorryworks.net/article50.phtml. Access date: August 1, 2008.

Baumeister, R. F. (1996). *Evil: Inside human violence and cruelty.* New York: Freeman.

Baumeister, R. F., Smart, L., & Boden, J. M. (1996). Relation of threatened egotism to violence and aggression: The dark side of high self-esteem. *Psychological Review, 103*, 5–33.

Bazerman, M. (2005). *Judgment in managerial decision making.* New York: Wiley.

Bennett, R. J., & Robinson, S. L. (2002). The past, present and future of deviance research. In J. Greenberg (Ed.), *Organizational behavior: The state of the science.* New York: Wiley.

Bergler, E. (1946). Poetic justice and its unconscious background. *Medical Record, 1*, 548–550.

Berkowitz, L. (1989). Frustration-aggression hypothesis: Examination and reformulation. *Psychological Bulletin, 106*, 59–73.

Berkowitz, L. (1993). *Aggression: Its causes, consequences, and control.* Philadelphia: Temple University Press.

Bies, R. J. (1987). The predicament of injustice: The management of moral outrage. In L. L. Cummings and B. M. Staw (Eds.), *Research in organizational behavior* (Vol. 9, pp. 289–319). Greenwich, CT: JAI Press.

Bies, R. J. (2008). Peering into the soul of discontent: Forgivable and unforgivable offenses. Working paper, McDonough School of Business, Georgetown University.

Bies, R. J., & Moag, J. S. (1986). Interactional justice: Communication criteria of fairness. In R. J. Lewicki, B. H. Sheppard, & M. H. Bazerman (Eds.), *Research on negotiation in organizations* (Vol. 1, pp. 43–55). Greenwich, CT: JAI Press.

Bies, R. J., & Tripp, T. M. (1995). The use and abuse of power: Justice as social control. In R. Cropanzano & M. Kacmar (Eds.), *Politics, justice, and support: Managing social climate at work* (pp. 131–146). Westport, CT: Quorum Press.

Bies, R. J., & Tripp, T. M. (1996). Beyond distrust: "Getting even" and the need for revenge. In R. M. Kramer & T. Tyler (Eds.), *Trust in organizations* (pp. 246–260). Thousand Oaks, CA: Sage.

Bies, R. J., & Tripp, T. M. (1998). The many faces of revenge: The good, the bad, and the ugly. In Samuel B. Bacharach (Series Ed.), *Monographs in Organizational Behavior and Relations*, Vol. 23: R. W. Griffin, A. O'Leary-Kelly, & J. Collins (Eds.), *Dysfunctional behavior in organizations, Part B, Non-violent dysfunctional behavior* (pp. 49–68). Greenwich, CT: JAI Press.

Bies, R. J., Tripp, T. M., & Kramer, R. M. (1997). At the breaking point: A social cognitive perspective on vengeance and violence in organizations. In R. A. Giacalone & J. Greenberg (Eds.), *Antisocial behavior in organizations* (pp. 18–36). Thousand Oaks, CA: Sage.

Bole, W. B., Christiansen, D., & Hennemeyer, R. T. (2004). *Forgiveness in international politics*. Washington, DC: USCCB Publishing.

Boraine, A. (2001). *A country unmasked: Inside South Africa's Truth and Reconciliation Commission*. New York: Oxford University Press.

Brackett, N. (2002, March). Roger Waters breathes easier. *Rolling Stone*.

Brief, A. P., & Weiss, H. M. (2002). Organizational behavior: Affect in the workplace. *Annual Review of Psychology, 53*, 279–307.

Bright, D. S., Fry, R. E., & Cooperrider, D. L. (2007). Forgiveness from the perspectives of three response modes: Begrudgement, pragmatism, and transcendence. *Journal of Management, Spirituality & Religion, 3*, 78–103.

Brockner, J., & Wiesenfeld, B. M. (1996). An integrative framework for explaining reactions to decisions: Interactive effects of outcomes and procedures. *Psychological Bulletin, 120*, 189–208.

Bureau of Labor Statistics. (2000). Fatal occupational injuries in the United States, 1995–1999: A chartbook. (Report 965). Washington,

DC: Author. Available online: www.bls.gov/opub/cfoichartbook/pdf/ entirereport.pdf. Access date: June 15, 2008.

Bushman, B. J., & Baumeister, R. F. (1998). Threatened egotism, narcissism, self-esteem, and direct and displaced aggression: Does self-love or self-hate lead to violence? *Journal of Personality and Social Psychology*, 75, 219–229.

Cahn, E. (1949). *The sense of injustice*. New York: New York University Press.

Caprara, G. V., Barbaranelli, C., & Zimbardo, P. G. (1996). Understanding the complexity of human aggression: Affective, cognitive, and social dimensions of individual differences in propensity toward aggression. *European Journal of Personality*, 10, 133–155.

Cloke, K. (1993). Revenge, forgiveness and the magic of mediation. *Mediation Quarterly*, 11, 67–78.

Colby, K. M. (1981). Modeling a paranoid mind. *Behavioral and Brain Sciences*, 4, 515–560.

Cole v. ArvinMeritor Inc., No. 03–73872 (E. D. Mich.).

Corrado, R. R., Cohen, I. M., Glackman, W., & Odgers, C. (2003). Serious and violent young offenders decisions to recidivate: An assessment of five sentencing models. *Crime & Delinquency*, 49, 179–200.

Crossley, C. D. (in press). Emotional and behavioral reactions to social undermining: A closer look at perceived offender motives. *Organizational Behavior and Human Decision Processes*.

Danger! Demolition in progress. (1999, December). *Mojo Magazine*.

Danow, D. K. (1995). Official and unofficial culture: Verbal art and the art of revenge. *Semiotica*, 106, 245–255.

DeCremer, D. (2007). *Advances in the psychology of justice and affect*. Greenwich, CT: Information Age.

Doctor's apology: Evidence or not? (2006, February 2). Provo, Utah, *Daily Herald*.

Dollard, J., Doob, L., Miller, N., Mowrer, Q., & Sears, R. (1939). *Frustration and aggression*. New Haven, CT: Yale University Press.

Douglas, S. C., Kiewitz, K., Martinko, M., Harvey, P., Kim, Y., & Chun, J. U. (2008). Cognitions, emotions, and evaluations: An elaboration likelihood model for workplace aggression. *Academy of Management Review*, 33, 425–451.

Douglas, S. C., & Martinko, M. J. (2001). Exploring the role of individual differences in the prediction of workplace aggression. *Journal of Applied Psychology*, 86, 547–559.

Eisenberg, N. (2000). Emotion, regulation, and moral development. *Annual Review of Psychology*, 51, 665–697.

Eisenberger, R., Lynch, P., Aselage, J., & Rohdieck, S. (2004). Who takes the most revenge? Individual differences in negative reciprocity norm endorsement. *Personality and Social Psychology Bulletin*, 30, 787–799.

Exline, J. J., Worthington, E. L., Jr., Hill, P., & McCullough, M. E. (2003). Forgiveness and justice: A research agenda for social and personality psychology. *Personality and Social Psychology Review, 7,* 337–348.

Fiske, S. T., & Taylor, S. E. (1991). *Social cognition.* New York: McGraw-Hill.

Fox, S., Bennett, R. J., Tripp, T. M., & Aquino, K. (2008). Why employees forgive their offenders: An empirical test of a typology of forgiveness motives. Working paper. Louisiana Tech University.

Frank, J. D. (1987). The drive for power and the nuclear arms race. *American Psychologist, 42,* 337–344.

Franzen, J. (1994, October 24). Lost in the mail. *New Yorker.*

Fremer, M. (2008, February). The swiftboating of audiophiles. Stereophile.com. Available online: www.stereophile.com/thinkpieces/021708swiftboat/. Access date: June 19, 2008.

Fricke, D. (1987, November). Pink Floyd: The inside story. *Rolling Stone.*

Gabarro, J. J., & Kotter, J. P. (1980). Managing your boss: A compatible relationship with your superior is essential to being effective in your job. *Harvard Business Review, 58,* 92–100.

Galaway, B., & Judson, J. (1996). *Restorative justice: International perspectives.* Monsey, NY: Criminal Justice Press.

Goldman, B. (2003). The application of referent cognitions theory to legal-claiming by terminated workers: The role of organizational justice and anger. *Journal of Management, 29,* 705–728.

Goodwin, R. N. (1995). Remembering America: A voice from the sixties. New York: HarperCollins.

Grantiz, N., & Loewy, D. (2007). Applying ethical theories: Interpreting and responding to student plagiarism. *Journal of Business Ethics, 72,* 293–306.

Greenberg, J. (1990). Employee theft as a reaction to underpayment inequity: The hidden costs of pay cuts. *Journal of Applied Psychology, 75,* 561–568.

Greenberg, J. (1990). Looking fair vs. being fair: Managing impressions of organizational justice. In L. L. Cummings & B. M. Staw (Eds.), *Research in organizational behavior* (Vol. 12, pp. 111–157). Greenwich, CT: JAI Press.

Greenberg, L., & Barling, J. (1999). Predicting employee aggression against coworkers, subordinates and supervisors: The roles of person behaviors and perceived workplace factors. *Journal of Organizational Behavior, 20,* 897–913.

Gregoire, Y., & Fisher, R. J. (2006). The effects of relationship quality on customer retaliation. *Marketing Letters, 17,* 31–46.

Guth, W., Schmittberger, R., & Schwarze, B. (1982). An experimental analysis of ultimatum bargaining. *Journal of Economic Behavior and Organization, 3,* 367–388.

Harlos, K. P., & Pinder, C. C. (2000). Emotion and injustice in the workplace. In S. Fineman (Ed.), *Emotion in organizations* (2nd ed., pp. 255–276). London: Sage.

Hastorf, A., & Cantril, H. (1954). They saw a game: A case study. *Journal of Abnormal Psychology, 49,* 129–134.

Heider, F. (1958). *The psychology of interpersonal relations.* New York: Wiley.

Hershcovis, S. M., Turner, N., Barling, J., Arnold, K. A., Dupré, K. E., Inness, M., LeBlanc, M. M., & Sivanathan, N. (2007). Predicting workplace aggression: A meta-analysis. *Journal of Applied Psychology, 92,* 228–238.

Hornstein, H. A. (1997). Brutal bosses and their prey: How to identify and overcome abuse in the workplace. New York: Riverhead Books.

Horowitz, M. J. (2007). Understanding and ameliorating revenge fantasies in psychotherapy. *American Journal of Psychiatry, 164,* 24–27.

Hovat, G., & London, M. (1980). Attributions of conflict management strategies in supervisor-subordinate dyads. *Journal of Applied Psychology, 65,* 172–175.

Israeli tit-for-tat death claims. (2005, June 3). BBC.com. Available online: http://news.bbc.co.uk/2/hi/middle_east/4605899.stm. Access date: June 18, 2008.

Jacoby, S. (1983). *Wild justice: The evolution of revenge.* New York: Harper-Collins.

Janis, I. L. (1983). *Groupthink* (2nd ed.). Boston: Houghton Mifflin.

Jones, D. A. (in press). Getting even for interpersonal mistreatment in the workplace: Triggers of revenge motives and behavior. In J. Greenberg (Ed.), *Insidious workplace behavior.* Hillsdale, NJ: Erlbaum.

Jones, D. A., & Skarlicki, D. P. (in press). How perceptions of fairness can change: A dynamic model of organizational justice. In J. Greenberg (Ed.), *Research in organizational justice* (Vol. 1). San Diego: Elsevier.

Jones, E. E., & Nisbett, R. E. (1972). The actor and the observer: Divergent perceptions of the causes of behavior. In E. E. Jones, D. E. Kanouse, H. H. Kelley, R. E. Nisbett, S. Valins, & B. Weiner (Eds.), *Attribution: Perceiving the causes of behavior* (pp. 79–94). Morristown, NJ: General Learning Press.

Kahn, R. L., & Kramer, R. M. (1990). Untying the knot: De-escalatory processes in international conflict. In R. L. Kahn & M. N. Zald (Eds.), *Organizations and nation-states: New perspectives on conflict and cooperation.* San Francisco: Jossey-Bass.

Kearns-Goodwin, D. (1991). *Lyndon Johnson and the American dream.* New York: St. Martin's Griffin.

Kelley, H. H. (1972). Attribution in social interaction. In E. E. Jones, D. E. Kanouse, H. H. Kelley, R. E. Nisbett, S. Valins, & B. Weiner (Eds.), *Attribution: Perceiving the causes of behavior* (pp. 1–26). Morristown, NJ: General Learning Press.

Kerr, S. (1995). On the folly of rewarding A, while hoping for B. *Academy of Management Executive, 9*, 7–14.

Kim, P. H., Dirks, K. T., Cooper, C. D., & Ferrin, D. L. (2006). When more blame is better than less: The implications of internal vs. external attributions for the repair of trust after a competence- vs. integrity-based trust violation. *Organizational Behavior and Human Decision Processes, 99*, 49–65.

Kim, P. H., Ferrin, D. L., Cooper, C. D., & Dirks, K. T. (2004). Removing the shadow of suspicion: The effects of apology vs. denial for repairing ability- vs. integrity-based trust violations. *Journal of Applied Psychology, 89*, 104–118.

Kim, S. H., Smith, R. H., & Brigham, N. L. (1998). Effects of power imbalance and the presence of third parties on reactions to harm: Upward and downward revenge. *Personality and Social Psychology Bulletin, 24*, 353–361.

Knowlton, W. A., & Mitchell, T. R. (1980). Effects of causal attributions on a supervisor's evaluation of subordinate performance. *Journal of Applied Psychology, 65*, 459–566.

Kraman, S. S., & Hamm, G. (1999). Risk management: Extreme honesty may be the best policy. *Annals of Internal Medicine, 131*, 963–967.

Kramer, R. M. (1994). The sinister attribution error. *Motivation and Emotion, 18*, 199–231.

Kramer, R. M. (1995). The distorted view from the top: Power, paranoia, and distrust in organizations. In R. Bies, R. Lewicki, & B. Sheppard (Eds.), *Research on negotiations in organizations* (Vol. 5). Greenwich, CT: JAI Press.

Kramer, R. M. (2001). Organizational paranoia: Origins and dynamics. In B. Staw & R. I. Sutton (Eds.), *Research in organizational behavior, 23*, 1–42.

Kramer, R. M. (2003, October). The harder they fall. *Harvard Business Review, 81*, 58–66.

Lelyveld, A. (1971). Punishment: For and against. In A. S. Neill (Ed.), *Punishment: For and against.* New York: Hart.

Lerner, J. S., & Keltner, D. (2000). Beyond valence: Toward a model of emotion-specific influences on judgment and choice. *Cognition and Emotion, 14*, 473–493.

Lerner, J. S., & Keltner, D. (2001). Fear, anger, and risk. *Journal of Personality and Personal Psychology, 81*, 146–159.

Leventhal, G. S. (1980). What should be done with equity theory? New approaches to the study of fairness in social relationships. In K. Gergen, M. Greenberg, & R. Willis (Eds.), *Social exchange: Advances in theory and research* (pp. 27–55). New York: Plenum Press.

Lewicki, R. J., Barry, B., & Saunders, D. M. (2006). *Negotiation* (5th ed.). Homewood, IL: Irwin.

Lind, A., & Tyler, T. R. (1988). *The social psychology of procedural justice*. New York: Plenum.

Lyubomirksy, S., & Nolen-Hoeksema, S. (1993). Self-perpetuating properties of dysphoric rumination. *Journal of Personality and Social Psychology, 65*, 339–349.

MacLean, P. A. (2006). Are companies bound by promises of life time benefits? *National Law Journal*. Available online: www.law.com/jsp/article .jsp?id = 1152608728017. Access date: June 16, 2008.

Man who posed as Marine hero sentenced to tend military graves. (2007, July 31). *Seattle Post-Intelligencer*.

Martinko, M. J., & Zellars, K. L. (1998). Toward a theory of workplace violence and aggression: A cognitive appraisal perspective. In Samuel B. Bacharach (Series Ed.), *Monographs in Organizational Behavior and Relations*, Vol. 23: R. W. Griffin, A. O'Leary-Kelly, & J. Collins (Eds.), *Dysfunctional behavior in organizations, Part A: Violent and deviant behavior* (pp. 1–42). Stamford, CT: JAI Press.

Mason, N. (2004). *Inside out: A personal history of Pink Floyd*. San Francisco: Chronicle Books.

Matthews, C. (1988). *Hardball*. New York: Summit Books.

Mayer, R. C., Davis, J. H., & Schoorman, D. F. (1995). An integrative model of organizational trust. *Academy of Management Review, 20*, 709–734.

McCullough, M. L. (2008). *Beyond revenge: The evolution of the forgiveness instinct*. San Francisco: Jossey-Bass.

McGregor, J. (2007, January 22). Sweet revenge: The power of retribution, spite, and loathing in the world of business. *Business Week*.

McGregor, J. (2008, March 3). Consumer vigilantes. *Business Week*.

McLean Parks, J. M. (1997). The fourth arm of justice: The art and science of revenge. In R. J. Lewicki, R. J. Bies, & B. H. Sheppard (Eds.), *Research on negotiation in organizations* (Vol. 6, pp. 113–144). Greenwich, CT: JAI Press.

Milgram, S. (1974). *Obedience to authority: An experimental view*. New York: HarperCollins.

Miller, D. T. (2001). Disrespect and the experience of injustice. *Annual Review of Psychology, 52*, 527–553.

Montville, J. V. (1993). The healing function of conflict resolution. In D. J. D. Sandole & H. van der Merwe (Eds.), *Conflict resolution: Theory and practice* (pp. 112–128). New York: Manchester University Press.

Morrill, C. (1996). *The executive way: Conflict management in corporations*. Chicago: University of Chicago Press.

National Center on Addiction and Substance Abuse at Columbia University. (2000). *The United States Postal Service Commission on a Safe and Secure Workplace*. New York: Author.

Neuman, J. H., & Baron, R. A. (1997). Aggression in the workplace. In R. A. Giacalone & J. Greenberg (Eds.), *Antisocial behavior in organizations* (pp. 37–67). Thousand Oaks, CA: Sage.

Neuman, J., & Baron, R. A. (1998). Workplace violence and workplace aggression: Evidence concerning specific forms, potential causes, and preferred targets. *Journal of Management, 24,* 391–419.

Ochs, J., & Roth, A. E. (1989). An experimental study of sequential bargaining. *American Economic Review, 79,* 335–385.

Pease, P. W., Schreiber, A. M., & Taylor, A. W. (2003). Caught telling the truth: Effects of honesty and communication media in distributive negotiations. *Group Decision and Negotiation, 12,* 537–566.

Peters, E., Vastfjall, D., Garling, T., & Slovic, P. (2006). Affect and decision making: A hot topic. *Journal of Behavioral Decision Making, 19,* 79–85.

Pfeffer, J. (1992). *Managing with power.* Boston: Harvard Business School Press.

Pyszczynski, T., & Greenberg, J. (1987). Self-regulatory perseveration and the depressive self-focusing style: A self-awareness theory of reactive depression. *Psychological Bulletin, 102,* 122–138.

Roger Waters talks new albums. (2000, November 27). *Billboard Magazine.*

Ross, L., & Nisbett, R. E. (1992). *The person and the situation.* New York: McGraw-Hill.

Rozenman, E. (2003, August 22). *USA Today,* "Tit-for-Tat" Editorial. The Committee on Accuracy in Middle East Reporting in America. Available online: www.camera.org/index.asp?x_context = 2&x_outlet = 53&x_article = 538. Access date: June 23, 2008.

Ruibal, S. (2008, January 31). Neuheisel scrambles to keep solid UCLA class together. *USA Today.*

Salmon, J. L. (2008). Pope watch. Available online: http://blog.washingtonpost.com/pope-watch/. Access date: June 23, 2008.

Sanfey, A. G., Rilling, J. K., Aronson, J. A., Nystrom, L. E., & Cohen, J. D. (2003). The neural basis of economic decision-making in the ultimatum game. *Science, 300,* 1755–1758.

Sashkin, M., & Williams, R. L. (1990). Does fairness make a difference? *Organizational Dynamics, 19,* 56–71.

Scott, W. G., & Hart, D. K. (1979). *Organizational America.* Boston: Houghton Mifflin.

Sheppard, B. H., Lewicki, R. J., & Minton, J. W. (1992). *Organizational justice: The search for fairness in the workplace.* New York: Lexington Books.

Simons, T., & Roberson, Q. (2003). Why managers should care about fairness: The effects of aggregate justice perceptions on organizational outcomes. *Journal of Applied Psychology, 88,* 432–443.

Skarlicki, D. P., Barclay, L. J., & Pugh, S. D. (2008). When explanations for layoffs are not enough: Employer's integrity as a moderator of the relationship between informational justice and retaliation. *Journal of Occupational and Organizational Psychology, 81,* 123–146.

Skarlicki, D. P., & Folger, R. (1997). Retaliation in the workplace: The roles of distributive, procedural, and interactional justice. *Journal of Applied Psychology, 82*, 434–443.

Skarlicki, D. P., Folger, R., & Tesluk, P. (1999). Personality as a moderator in the relationship between fairness and retaliation. *Academy of Management Journal, 42*, 100–108.

Solomon, R. C. (1990). *A passion for justice: Emotions and the origins of the social contract.* Reading, MA: Addison-Wesley.

Stouten, J., De Cremer, D., & van Dijk, E. (2006). Violating equality in social dilemmas: Emotional and retributive reactions as a function of trust, attribution, and honesty. *Personality and Social Psychology Bulletin, 32*, 894–906.

Sutton, R. I. (2007). *The no asshole rule: Building a civilized workplace and surviving one that isn't.* New York: Warner Business.

Swisher, K. (1994, May 8). Working under the gun. *Washington Post*, p. H1.

Takaku, S. (2001). The effects of apology and perspective taking on interpersonal forgiveness: A dissonance-attribution model of interpersonal forgiveness. *Journal of Social Psychology, 141*, 494–508.

Thomas, K. W., & Pondy, L. R. (1977). Toward an "intent" model of conflict management among principal parties. *Human Relations, 30*, 1089–1102.

Thomas, K. W., & Schmidt, W. H. (1976). A survey of managerial interests with respect to conflict. *Academy of Management Journal, 19*, 315–318.

Tjosvold, D. (2008). The conflict-positive organization: It depends on us. *Journal of Organizational Behavior, 29*, 19–28.

Tjosvold, D., & Chia, L. C. (1989). Conflict between managers and workers: The role of cooperation and competition. *Journal of Social Psychology, 129*, 235–247.

Tripp, T. M. (1993). Power and fairness in negotiations. *Social Justice Research, 6*, 19–39.

Tripp, T. M., & Bies, R. J. (1997). What's good about revenge? In R. J. Lewicki, R. J. Bies, and B. H. Sheppard (Eds.), *Research on negotiation in organizations* (Vol. 6, pp. 145–160). Greenwich, CT: JAI Press.

Tripp, T. M., & Bies, R. J. (in press). "Righteous" anger and revenge in the workplace: The fantasies, the feuds, the forgiveness. In M. Potegal & G. Stemmler (Eds.), *A handbook of anger: Constituent and concomitant biological, psychological, and social processes.* Amsterdam: Springer.

Tripp, T. M., Bies, R. J., & Aquino, K. (2002). Poetic justice or petty jealousy? The aesthetics of revenge. *Organizational Behavior and Human Decision Processes, 89*, 966–984.

Tripp, T. M., Bies, R. J., & Aquino, K. (2007). A vigilante model of justice: Revenge, reconciliation, forgiveness, and avoidance. *Social Justice Research, 19*, 10–34.

Wall, J. A., & Callister, R. R. (1995). Conflict and its management. *Journal of Management, 21,* 515–558.

Wason, P. (1960). On the failure to eliminate hypotheses in a conceptual task. *Quarterly Journal of Experimental Psychology, 12,* 129–140.

Weick, K. E. (1995). *Sensemaking in organizations.* Thousand Oaks, CA: Sage.

Weiner, B. (1995). *Judgments of responsibility.* New York: Guilford Press.

Wilson, T. D., & Kraft, D. (1993). Why do I love thee? Effects of repeated introspections about a dating relationship on attitudes towards the relationship. *Personality and Social Psychology Bulletin, 19,* 409–418.

Wintz, J. (2004). Archbishop Sean P. O'Malley: A new voice in Boston. *St. Anthony Messenger.* Available online: www.americancatholic.org/Messenger/Mar2004/Feature1.asp. Access date: June 23, 2008.

Witvliet, C. V. O., Worthington, E. L., Root, L. M., Sato, A. M., Ludwig, T. E., & Exline, J. J. (2008). Retributive justice, restorative justice, and forgiveness: An experimental psychophysiology analysis. *Journal of Experimental Social Psychology, 44,* 10–25.

Wong, P. T., & Weiner, B. (1981). When people ask "why" questions, and the heuristics of attributional search. *Journal of Personality and Social Psychology, 40,* 650–663.

Woodstock Theological Center. (1998). *Forgiveness and conflict resolution: Reality and utility.* Washington, DC: Woodstock Center.

Worthington, E., & Scherer, M. (2004). Forgiveness is an emotion-focused coping strategy that can reduce health risks and promote health resilience: Theory, review, and hypotheses. *Psychology and Health, 19,* 385–405.

Worthington, E. L., Witvliet, C. V. O., Pietrini, P., & Miller, A. J. (2007). Forgiveness, health, and well-being: A review of evidence for emotional versus decisional forgiveness, dispositional forgivingness, and reduced unforgiveness. *Journal of Behavioral Medicine, 30,* 291–302.

Notes

Chapter One

1. Allen, M. (2001, June 3). Bush aide details alleged Clinton staff vandalism. *Washington Post*, p. A01. Available online: www.papillonsartpalace.com/trashing.htm. Access date: June 15, 2008.
2. Aquino, K., Tripp, T. M., & Bies, R. J. (2001). How employees respond to personal offense: The effects of blame attribution, victim status, and offender status on revenge and reconciliation in the workplace. *Journal of Applied Psychology*, 86, 52–59.
3. Jacoby, S. (1983). *Wild justice: The evolution of revenge*. New York: HarperCollins.
4. Neuman, J., & Baron, R. A. (1998). Workplace violence and workplace aggression: Evidence concerning specific forms, potential causes, and preferred targets. *Journal of Management, 24*, 391–419.
5. Neuman & Baron (1998).
6. Bureau of Labor Statistics. (2000). *Fatal occupational injuries in the United States, 1995–1999: A chartbook*. (Report 965). Washington, DC: Author. Available online: www.bls.gov/opub/cfoichartbook/pdf/entirereport.pdf. Access date: June 15, 2008.
7. Neuman & Baron (1998).

8. Swisher, K. (1994, May 8). Working under the gun. *Washington Post*, p. H1.

9. The National Center on Addiction and Substance Abuse at Columbia University. (2000). *The United States Postal Service Commission on a Safe and Secure Workplace*. New York: Author.

10. Tripp, T. M., & Bies, R. J. (in press). "Righteous" anger and revenge in the workplace: The fantasies, the feuds, the forgiveness. In M. Potegal & G. Stemmler (Eds.), *A handbook of anger: Constituent and concomitant biological, psychological, and social processes*. Amsterdam: Springer.

11. Bies, R. J., & Tripp, T. M. (1998). The many faces of revenge: The good, the bad, and the ugly. In Samuel B. Bacharach (Series Ed.), *Monographs in organizational behavior and relations*, Vol. 23: R. W. Griffin, A. O'Leary-Kelly, & J. Collins (Eds.), *Dysfunctional behavior in organizations, Part B, Non-violent dysfunctional behavior* (pp. 49–68). Greenwich, CT: JAI Press.

12. Axelrod, R. (1997). *The complexity of cooperation: Agent-based models of competition and collaboration*. Princeton, NJ: Princeton University Press.

13. Axelrod, R. (1984). *The evolution of cooperation*. New York: Basic Books; McCullough, M. L. (2008). *Beyond revenge: The evolution of the forgiveness instinct*. San Francisco: Jossey-Bass.

14. Bies, R. J., & Tripp, T. M. (1995). *The use and abuse of power: Justice as social control*. In R. Cropanzano & M. Kacmar (Eds.), *Politics, justice, and support: Managing social climate at work* (pp. 131–146). Westport, CT: Quorum Press; Bies, R. J. (1987). The predicament of injustice: The management of moral outrage. In L. L. Cummings & B. M. Staw (Eds.), *Research in organizational behavior* (Vol. 9, pp. 289–319). Greenwich, CT: JAI Press; Cahn, E. (1949). *The sense of injustice*. New York: New York University Press; Solomon, R. C. (1990). *A passion for justice: Emotions and the origins of the social contract*. Reading, MA: Addison-Wesley.

15. McCullough (2008).

16. Thomas, K. W., & Schmidt, W. H. (1976). A survey of managerial interests with respect to conflict. *Academy of Management Journal, 19,* 315–318.

17. Hovat, G., & London, M. (1980). Attributions of conflict management strategies in supervisor-subordinate dyads. *Journal of Applied Psychology, 65,* 172–175.

18. Tjosvold, D. (2008). The conflict-positive organization: It depends on us. *Journal of Organizational Behavior, 29,* 19–28.

19. For a review, see Lind, A., & Tyler, T. R. (1988). *The social psychology of procedural justice.* New York: Plenum. For an application to workplace settings, see Sheppard, B. H., Lewicki, R. J., & Minton, J. W. (1992). *Organizational justice: The search for fairness in the workplace.* New York: Lexington Books.

20. Fiske, S. T., & Taylor, S. E. (1991). *Social cognition.* New York: McGraw-Hill.

21. Berkowitz, L. (1993). *Aggression: Its causes, consequences, and control.* Philadelphia: Temple University Press.

22. McCullough (2008).

23. Bennett, R. J., & Robinson, S. L. (2002). The past, present and future of deviance research. In J. Greenberg (Ed.), *Organizational behavior: The state of the science.* New York: Wiley.

24. Bies, R. J., & Tripp, T. M. (1998). Two faces of the powerless: Coping with tyranny. In R. M. Kramer & M. A. Neale (Eds.), *Power and influence in organizations* (pp. 203–220). Thousand Oaks, CA: Sage; Jacoby (1983); McLean Parks, J. M. (1997). *The fourth arm of justice: The art and science of revenge.* In R. J. Lewicki, R. J. Bies, & B. H. Sheppard (Eds.), *Research on negotiation in organizations* (Vol. 6, pp. 113–144). Greenwich, CT: JAI Press.

25. Sashkin, M., & Williams, R. L. (1990). Does fairness make a difference? *Organizational Dynamics, 19,* 56–71.

Chapter Two

1. McGregor, J. (2007, January 22). Sweet revenge: The power of retribution, spite, and loathing in the world of business. *Business Week*.
2. McGregor (2007).
3. McGregor (2007).
4. Scott, W. G., & Hart, D. K. (1979). *Organizational America*. Boston: Houghton Mifflin.
5. Neuman, J., & Baron, R. A. (1998). Workplace violence and workplace aggression: Evidence concerning specific forms, potential causes, and preferred targets. *Journal of Management, 24*, 391–419.
6. Greenberg, L., & Barling, J. (1999). Predicting employee aggression against coworkers, subordinates and supervisors: The roles of person behaviors and perceived workplace factors. *Journal of Organizational Behavior, 20*, 897–913.
7. Banaji, M. R., Bazerman, M. H., & Chugh, D. (2003). How (un)ethical are you? *Harvard Business Review, 81*, 56–64. See also Baumeister, R. F. (1996). *Evil: Inside human violence and cruelty*. New York: Freeman.
8. For instance, in the world of student cheating, see Grantiz, N., & Loewy, D. (2007). Applying ethical theories: Interpreting and responding to student plagiarism. *Journal of Business Ethics, 72*, 293–306.
9. Bies, R. J., & Tripp, T. M. (1998). Two faces of the powerless: Coping with tyranny. In R. M. Kramer & M. A. Neale (Eds.), *Power and influence in organizations* (pp. 203–220). Thousand Oaks, CA: Sage.
10. For a slight variation on categories of triggers, see Jones, D. A. (in press). Getting even for interpersonal mistreatment in the workplace: Triggers of revenge motives and behavior. In J. Greenberg (Ed.), *Insidious workplace behavior*. Hillsdale, NJ: Erlbaum.
11. McGregor (2007); Jacoby, S. (1983). *Wild justice: The evolution of revenge*. New York: HarperCollins.

12. Jacoby (1983).
13. McCullough, M. L. (2008). *Beyond revenge: The evolution of the forgiveness instinct*. San Francisco: Jossey-Bass.
14. Jacoby (1983), pp. 4–5.
15. Tripp, T. M., & Bies, R. J. (1997). What's good about revenge? The avenger's perspective. In R. J. Lewicki, R. J. Bies, & B. H. Sheppard (Eds.), *Research on negotiation in organizations* (Vol. 6, pp. 145–160). Greenwich, CT: JAI Press.
16. Bies & Tripp (1998).
17. Bies, R. J., Tripp, T. M., & Kramer, R. M. (1997). At the breaking point: A social cognitive perspective on vengeance and violence in organizations. In R. A. Giacalone & J. Greenberg (Eds.), *Antisocial behavior in organizations* (pp. 18–36). Thousand Oaks, CA: Sage; Kramer, R. M. (1994). The sinister attribution error. *Motivation and Emotion, 18*, 199–231.
18. Bies, Tripp, & Kramer (1997).
19. Horowitz, M. J. (2007). Understanding and ameliorating revenge fantasies in psychotherapy. *American Journal of Psychiatry, 164*, 24–27.
20. Matthews, C. (1988). *Hardball*. New York: Summit Books, p. 111.
21. Aquino, K., Tripp, T. M., & Bies, R. J. (2006). Getting even or moving on? Power, procedural justice, and types of offense as predictors of revenge, forgiveness, reconciliation, and avoidance in organizations. *Journal of Applied Psychology, 91*, 653–658. See also Tripp, T. M., Bies, R. J., & Aquino, K. (2007). A vigilante model of justice: Revenge, reconciliation, forgiveness, and avoidance. *Social Justice Research, 19*, 10–34.

Chapter Three

1. Dollard, J., Doob, L., Miller, N., Mowrer, O., & Sears, R. (1939). *Frustration and aggression*. New Haven, CT: Yale University Press; Berkowitz, L. (1989). Frustration-aggression hypothesis: Examination and reformulation. *Psychological Bulletin, 106*, 59–73.

2. Berkowitz (1989). See also Caprara, G. V., Barbaranelli, C., & Zimbardo, P. G. (1996). Understanding the complexity of human aggression: Affective, cognitive, and social dimensions of individual differences in propensity toward aggression. *European Journal of Personality, 10,* 133–155.

3. Morrill, C. (1996). *The executive way: Conflict management in corporations*. Chicago: University of Chicago Press.

4. MacLean, P. A. (2006, July 12). Are companies bound by promises of lifetime benefits? *National Law Journal*. Available online: www.law.com/jsp/article.jsp?id=1152608728017. Access date: June 16, 2008.

5. *Cole v. ArvinMeritor Inc.,* No. 03–73872 (E.D. Mich.).

6. Bies, R. J., & Tripp, T. M. (1996). Beyond distrust: "Getting even" and the need for revenge. In R. M. Kramer & T. Tyler (Eds.), *Trust in organizations* (pp. 246–260). Thousand Oaks, CA: Sage.

7. Sutton, R. I. (2007). *The no asshole rule: Building a civilized workplace and surviving one that isn't*. New York: Warner Business; Hornstein, H. A. (1997). *Brutal bosses and their prey: How to identify and overcome abuse in the workplace*. New York: Riverhead Books.

8. Ruibal, S. (2008, January 31). Neuheisel scrambles to keep solid UCLA class together. *USA Today*.

9. Aquino, K., Tripp, T. M., & Bies, R. J. (2006). Getting even or moving on? Power, procedural justice, and types of offense as predictors of revenge, forgiveness, reconciliation, and avoidance in organizations. *Journal of Applied Psychology, 91,* 653–658.

10. Skarlicki, D. P., & Folger, R. (1997). Retaliation in the workplace: The roles of distributive, procedural, and interactional justice. *Journal of Applied Psychology, 82,* 434–443.

11. For a review, see Lind, A., & Tyler, T. R. (1988). *The social psychology of procedural justice*. New York: Plenum. For an application to workplace settings, see Sheppard, B. H., Lewicki, R. J., & Minton, J. W. (1992). *Organizational*

justice: The search for fairness in the workplace. New York: Lexington Books.

12. Leventhal, G. S. (1980). What should be done with equity theory? New approaches to the study of fairness in social relationships. In K. Gergen, M. Greenberg, & R. Willis (Eds.), *Social exchange: Advances in theory and research* (pp. 27–55). New York: Plenum Press.

13. Bies, R. J., & Moag, J. S. (1986). Interactional justice: Communication criteria of fairness. In R. J. Lewicki, B. H. Sheppard, & M. H. Bazerman (Eds.), *Research on negotiation in organizations* (Vol. 1, pp. 43–55). Greenwich, CT: JAI Press.

Chapter Four

1. See Weick, K. E. (1995). *Sensemaking in organizations.* Thousand Oaks, CA: Sage. See also Fiske, S. T., & Taylor, S. E. (1991). *Social cognition.* New York: McGraw-Hill.

2. Hastorf, A., & Cantril, H. (1954). They saw a game: A case study. *Journal of Abnormal Psychology, 49,* 129–134.

3. Hastorf & Cantril (1954), p. 133.

4. For a readable discussion of how many of the biases that create these errors are unconscious, see Bazerman, M. (2005). *Judgment in managerial decision making.* New York: Wiley.

5. Weiner, B. (1995). *Judgments of responsibility.* New York: Guilford Press.

6. Allred, K. G. (1999). Anger driven retaliation: Toward an understanding of impassioned conflict in organizations. In R. J. Bies, R. J. Lewicki, & B. H. Sheppard (Eds.), *Research on negotiations in organizations* (Vol. 7, pp. 27–58). Greenwich, CT: JAI Press.

7. Neuman, J. H., & Baron, R. A. (1997). Aggression in the workplace. In R. A. Giacalone & J. Greenberg (Eds.), *Antisocial behavior in organizations* (pp. 37–67). Thousand Oaks, CA: Sage; Thomas, K. W., & Pondy, L. R. (1977).

Toward an "intent" model of conflict management among principal parties. *Human Relations, 30,* 1089–1102.

8. Wong, P. T., & Weiner, B. (1981). When people ask "why" questions, and the heuristics of attributional search. *Journal of Personality and Social Psychology, 40,* 650–663.

9. Bies, R. J., & Tripp, T. M. (1996). Beyond distrust: "Getting even" and the need for revenge. In R. M. Kramer & T. Tyler (Eds.), *Trust in organizations* (pp. 246–260). Thousand Oaks, CA: Sage.

10. Crossley, C. D. (in press). Emotional and behavioral reactions to social undermining: A closer look at perceived offender motives. *Organizational Behavior and Human Decision Processes.*

11. Morrill, C. (1992). Vengeance among executives. *Virginia Review of Sociology, 1,* 51–76.

12. Kramer, R. M. (1994). The sinister attribution error. *Motivation and Emotion, 18,* 199–231.

13. Bies & Tripp (1996).

14. See Kelley, H. H. (1972). Attribution in social interaction. In E. E. Jones, D. E. Kanouse, H. H. Kelley, R. E. Nisbett, S. Valins, & B. Weiner (Eds.), *Attribution: Perceiving the causes of behavior* (pp. 1–26). Morristown, NJ: General Learning Press.

15. Goldman, B. (2003). The application of referent cognitions theory to legal-claiming by terminated workers: The role of organizational justice and anger. *Journal of Management, 29,* 705–728.

16. Weick (1995); Bazerman (2005).

17. Kramer (1994).

18. Bazerman (2005).

19. Bies, R. J., Tripp, T. M., & Kramer, R. M. (1997). At the breaking point: Cognitive and social dynamics of revenge in organizations. In R. A. Giacalone & J. Greenberg (Eds.), *Antisocial behavior in organizations* (pp. 18–36). Thousand Oaks, CA: Sage.

20. Bies, Tripp, & Kramer (1997).
21. Bies, Tripp, & Kramer (1997); Janis, I. L. (1983). *Groupthink* (2nd ed.). Boston: Houghton Mifflin.
22. Kramer, R. M. (1995). The distorted view from the top: Power, paranoia, and distrust in organizations. In R. Bies, R. Lewicki, & B. Sheppard (Eds.), *Research on negotiations in organizations* (Vol. 5). Greenwich, CT: JAI Press.
23. For example, see Janis (1983); Weick (1995); and Pfeffer, J. (1992). *Managing with power*. Boston: Harvard Business School Press.
24. Janis (1983).
25. Pyszczynski, T., & Greenberg, J. (1987). Self-regulatory perseveration and the depressive self focusing style: A self-awareness theory of reactive depression. *Psychological Bulletin, 102*, 122–138; Lyubomirksy, S., & Nolen-Hoeksema, S. (1993). Self-perpetuating properties of dysphoric rumination. *Journal of Personality and Social Psychology, 65*, 339–349; Kramer, (1995).
26. Wilson, T. D., & Kraft, D. (1993). Why do I love thee? Effects of repeated introspections about a dating relationship on attitudes towards the relationship. *Personality and Social Psychology Bulletin, 19*, 409–418
27. Kramer, R. M. (2001). Organizational paranoia: Origins and dynamics. In B. Staw & R. I. Sutton (Eds.), *Research in organizational behavior, 23*, 1–42.
28. Colby, K. M. (1981). Modeling a paranoid mind. *Behavioral and Brain Sciences, 4*, 515–560.
29. Bies, Tripp, & Kramer (1997), p. 24; Kearns-Goodwin, D. (1991). *Lyndon Johnson and the American dream*. New York: St. Martin's Griffin, p. 316.
30. Jones, E. E., & Nisbett, R. E. (1972). The actor and the observer: Divergent perceptions of the causes of behavior. In E. E. Jones, D. E. Kanouse, H. H. Kelley, R. E. Nisbett, S. Valins, & B. Weiner (Eds.), *Attribution: Perceiving the*

causes of behavior (pp. 79–94). Morristown, NJ: General Learning Press.

31. Knowlton, W. A., & Mitchell, T. R. (1980). Effects of causal attributions on a supervisor's evaluation of sub-ordinate performance. *Journal of Applied Psychology, 65,* 459–566.

32. Kramer (1994, 1995).

33. Kramer (1994, 1995).

34. Goodwin, R. N. (1995). *Remembering America: A voice from the sixties.* New York: HarperCollins.

35. Goodwin (1995), p. 55.

36. Wason, P. (1960). On the failure to eliminate hypotheses in a conceptual task. *Quarterly Journal of Experimental Psychology, 12,* 129–140; Hastorf & Cantril (1954).

37. Wason (1960).

38. Morrill (1992).

39. Goldman (2003).

40. Ross, L., & Nisbett, R. E. (1992). *The person and the situation.* New York: McGraw-Hill.

41. For example, see Asch, S. (1951). Effects of group pressure upon the modification and distortion of judgment. In H. Guetzkow (Ed.), *Groups, leadership, and men* (pp. 177–190). Pittsburgh: Carnegie Press.

42. Bies, R. J. (1987). The predicament of injustice: The management of moral outrage. In L. L. Cummings & B. M. Staw (Eds.), *Research in organizational behavior* (Vol. 9, pp. 289–319). Greenwich, CT: JAI Press.

43. Goldman (2003).

44. Kramer (1995).

45. Frank, J. D. (1987). The drive for power and the nuclear arms race. *American Psychologist, 42,* 337–344; quote on p. 340, emphasis added.

46. Tripp, T. M., & Bies, R. J. (1997). What's good about revenge? The avenger's perspective. In R. J. Lewicki, R. J. Bies, & B. H. Sheppard (Eds.), *Research on negotiation in*

organizations (Vol. 6, pp. 145–160). Greenwich, CT: JAI Press.

47. Kahn, R. L., & Kramer, R. M. (1990). Untying the knot: De-escalatory processes in international conflict. In R. L. Kahn & M. N. Zald (Eds.), *Organizations and nation-states: New perspectives on conflict and cooperation*. San Francisco: Jossey-Bass.

48. Bole, W. B., Christiansen, D., & Hennemeyer, R. T. (2004). *Forgiveness in international politics*. Washington, DC: USCCB Publishing.

49. McGregor, J. (2007, January 22). Sweet revenge. *Business Week*.

50. Tjosvold, D., & Chia, L. C. (1989). Conflict between managers and workers: The role of cooperation and competition. *Journal of Social Psychology, 129*, 235–247; Wall, J. A., & Callister, R. R. (1995). Conflict and its management. *Journal of Management, 21*, 515–558.

51. Douglas, S. C., Kiewitz, K., Martinko, M., Harvey, P., Kim, Y., & Chun, J. U. (2008). Cognitions, emotions, and evaluations: An elaboration likelihood model for workplace aggression. *Academy of Management Review, 33*, 425–451.

52. Morrill, (1992).

53. For instance, see al-Mugahbri, N. (2004, June 30). Tit-for-tat raid after fatal rocket attack. *Sydney Morning Herald*. Available online: www.smh.com.au/articles/2004/06/29/1088487964342.html?from=storylhs. Access date: June 18, 2008. See also Israeli tit-for-tat death claims. (2005, June 3). BBC.com. Available online: http://news.bbc.co.uk/2/hi/middle_east/4605899.stm. Access date: June 18, 2008.

54. Fricke, D. (1987, November). Pink Floyd: The inside story. *Rolling Stone*.

55. Mason, N. (2004). *Inside out: A personal history of Pink Floyd*. San Francisco: Chronicle Books, p. 280.

56. Danger! Demolition in progress. (1999, December). *Mojo Magazine*.

57. Fricke (1987).
58. Brackett, N. (2002, March). Roger Waters breathes easier. *Rolling Stone*.
59. Roger Waters talks new albums. (2000, November 27). *Billboard Magazine*.

Chapter Five

1. DeCremer, D. (2007). *Advances in the psychology of justice and affect*. Greenwich, CT: Information Age. Lerner, J. S., & Keltner, D. (2000). Beyond valence: Toward a model of emotion-specific influences on judgment and choice. *Cognition and Emotion, 14*, 473–493. See also Peters, E., Vastfjall, D., Garling, T., & Slovic, P. (2006). Affect and decision making: A hot topic. *Journal of Behavioral Decision Making, 19*, 79–85.

2. Brief, A. P., & Weiss, H. M. (2002). Organizational behavior: Affect in the workplace. *Annual Review of Psychology, 53*, 279–307. See also Harlos, K. P., & Pinder, C. C. (2000). Emotion and injustice in the workplace. In S. Fineman (Ed.), *Emotion in organizations* (2nd ed., pp. 255–276). London: Sage.

3. Brief & Weiss (2002); Harlos & Pinder (2000).

4. Matthews, C. (1988). *Hardball*. New York: Summit Books, p. 107.

5. Sanfey, A. G., Rilling, J. K., Aronson, J. A., Nystrom, L. E., & Cohen, J. D. (2003). The neural basis of economic decision-making in the ultimatum game. *Science, 300*, 1755–1758.

6. Ochs, J., & Roth, A. E. (1989). An experimental study of sequential bargaining. *American Economic Review, 79*, 335–385.

7. Guth, W., Schmittberger, R., & Schwarze, B. (1982). An experimental analysis of ultimatum bargaining. *Journal of Economic Behavior and Organization, 3*, 367–388.

8. Guth, Schmittberger, & Schwarze (1982), p. 1758.

9. For a recent study that shows that injustice leads to blame, which leads to anger and then retaliation, see Barclay, L. J., Skarlicki, D. P., & Pugh, S. D. (2005). Exploring the role of emotions in injustice perceptions and retaliation. *Journal of Applied Psychology, 90*, 629–643. For reviews, see Eisenberg, N. (2000). Emotion, regulation, and moral development. *Annual Review of Psychology, 51*, 665–697; Miller, D. T. (2001). Disrespect and the experience of injustice. *Annual Review of Psychology, 52*, 527–553; and Anderson, C. A., & Bushman, B. J. (2002). Human aggression. *Annual Review of Psychology, 53*, 27–51.

10. Jones, D. A., & Skarlicki, D. P. (in press). How perceptions of fairness can change: A dynamic model of organizational justice. In J. Greenberg (Ed.), *Research in organizational justice* (Vol. 1). San Diego: Elsevier.

11. Cahn, E. (1949). *The sense of injustice*. New York: New York University Press, p. 13.

12. Cahn (1949).

13. Cahn (1949), p. 24.

Chapter Six

1. Horowitz, M. J. (2007). Understanding and ameliorating revenge fantasies in psychotherapy. *American Journal of Psychiatry, 164*, 24–27.

2. Franzen, J. (1994, October 24). Lost in the mail. *New Yorker*, p. 70.

3. Adams, J. S. (1965). Inequity in social exchange. In L. Berkowitz (Ed.), *Advances in experimental social psychology* (Vol. 2, pp. 267–299). New York: Academic Press. See also Adams, J. S., & Freedman, S. (1976). Equity theory revisited: Comments and annotated bibliography. In L. Berkowitz (Ed.), *Advances in experimental social psychology* (Vol. 9, pp. 43–90). New York: Academic Press.

4. McGregor, J. (2007, January 22). Sweet revenge: The power of retribution, spite, and loathing in the world of business. *Business Week*.

5. Gregoire, Y., & Fisher, R. J. (2006). The effects of relationship quality on customer retaliation. *Marketing Letters, 17*, 31–46.

6. McGregor, J. (2008, March 3). Consumer vigilantes. *Business Week*.

7. Fremer, M. (2008, February). The swiftboating of audiophiles. Stereophile.com. Available online: www.stereophile.com/thinkpieces/021708swiftboat/. Access date: June 19, 2008.

8. Simons, T., & Roberson, Q. (2003). Why managers should care about fairness: The effects of aggregate justice perceptions on organizational outcomes. *Journal of Applied Psychology, 88*, 432–443.

9. Greenberg, J. (1990). Employee theft as a reaction to underpayment inequity: The hidden costs of pay cuts. *Journal of Applied Psychology, 75*, 561–568.

10. Browning, V., personal communication with Tom Tripp, 2007.

11. Barreca, R. (1995). *Sweet revenge: The wicked delights of getting even*. New York: Harmony Books.

12. Hershcovis, S. M., Turner, N., Barling, J., Arnold, K. A., Dupré, K. E., Inness, M., LeBlanc, M. M., & Sivanathan, N. (2007). Predicting workplace aggression: A meta-analysis. *Journal of Applied Psychology, 92*, 228–238.

13. Hershcovis et al. (2007). Also, Douglas, S. C., & Martinko, M. J. (2001). Exploring the role of individual differences in the prediction of workplace aggression. *Journal of Applied Psychology, 86*, 547–559; and Eisenberger, R., Lynch, P., Aselage, J., & Rohdieck, S. (2004). Who takes the most revenge? Individual differences in negative reciprocity norm endorsement. *Personality and Social Psychology Bulletin, 30*, 787–799.

14. Skarlicki, D. P., Folger, R., & Tesluk, P. (1999). Personality as a moderator in the relationship between fairness and retaliation. *Academy of Management Journal, 42,* 100–108; Hershcovis et al. (2007).

15. Baumeister, R. F., Smart, L., & Boden, J. M. (1996). Relation of threatened egotism to violence and aggression: The dark side of high self-esteem. *Psychological Review, 103,* 5–33; Bushman, B. J., & Baumeister, R. F. (1998). Threatened egotism, narcissism, self-esteem, and direct and displaced aggression: Does self-love or self-hate lead to violence? *Journal of Personality and Social Psychology, 75,* 219–229; Anderson, C. A., & Bushman, B. J. (2002). Human aggression. *Annual Review of Psychology, 53,* 27–51.

16. Aquino, K., Douglas, S., & Martinko, M. J. (2003). Overt anger in response to victimization: Attributional style and organizational norms as moderators. *Journal of Occupational Health Psychology, 9,* 152–164.

17. Eisenberger, R., Lynch, P., Aselage, J., & Rohdieck, S. (2004). Who takes the most revenge? Individual differences in negative reciprocity norm endorsement. *Personality and Social Psychology Bulletin, 30,* 787–799.

18. Lerner, J. S., & Keltner, D. (2000). Beyond valence: Toward a model of emotion-specific influences on judgment and choice. *Cognition and Emotion, 14,* 473–493. Lerner, J. S., & Keltner, D. (2001). Fear, anger, and risk. *Journal of Personality and Personal Psychology, 81,* 146–159. Douglas, S. C., & Martinko, M. J. (2001). Exploring the role of individual differences in the prediction of workplace aggression. *Journal of Applied Psychology, 86,* 547–559.

19. Douglas, S. C., & Martinko, M. J. (2001). Exploring the role of individual differences in the prediction of workplace aggression. *Journal of Applied Psychology, 86,* 547–559.

20. Aquino, K., Tripp, T. M., & Bies, R. J. (2001). How employees respond to personal offense: The effects of blame attribution, victim status, and offender status on revenge

and reconciliation in the workplace. *Journal of Applied Psychology*, *86*, 52–59; Aquino, K., Tripp, T. M., & Bies, R. J. (2006). Getting even or moving on? Status variables and procedural justice as predictors of revenge, forgiveness, and reconciliation in organizations. *Journal of Applied Psychology*, *91*, 653–668.

21. Aquino, K., & Douglas, S. (2003). Identity threat and anti-social behavior in organizations: The moderating effects of individual differences, aggressive modeling, and hierarchical status. *Organizational Behavior and Human Decision Processes*, *90*, 195–208.

22. McCullough, M. L. (2008). *Beyond revenge: The evolution of the forgiveness instinct*. San Francisco: Jossey-Bass.

23. Aquino, Tripp, & Bies (2001); Kim, S. H., Smith, R. H., & Brigham, N. L. (1998). Effects of power imbalance and the presence of third parties on reactions to harm: Upward and downward revenge. *Personality and Social Psychology Bulletin*, *24*, 353–361.

24. Aquino, Tripp, & Bies (2001); Aquino, Tripp, & Bies (2006).

25. Bies, R. J., & Tripp, T. M. (1998). Two faces of the powerless: Coping with tyranny. In R. M. Kramer & M. A. Neale (Eds.), *Power and influence in organizations* (pp. 203–220). Thousand Oaks, CA: Sage.

Chapter Seven

1. Greenberg, J. (1990). Looking fair vs. being fair: Managing impressions of organizational justice. In L. L. Cummings & B. M. Staw (Eds.), *Research in organizational behavior* (Vol. 12, pp. 111–157). Greenwich, CT: JAI Press.

2. Brockner, J., & Wiesenfeld, B. M. (1996). An integrative framework for explaining reactions to decisions: Interactive effects of outcomes and procedures. *Psychological Bulletin*, *120*, 189–208. Or, at least, as a recent study shows, they are less likely to be moved to revenge when they perceive that

the manager has integrity; see Skarlicki, D. P., Barclay, L. J., & Pugh, S. D. (2008). When explanations for layoffs are not enough: Employer's integrity as a moderator of the relationship between informational justice and retaliation. *Journal of Occupational and Organizational Psychology, 81*, 123–146.

3. Tripp, T. M. (1993). Power and fairness in negotiations. *Social Justice Research, 6*, 19–39.

4. McCullough, M. L. (2008). *Beyond revenge: The evolution of the forgiveness instinct*. San Francisco: Jossey-Bass.

5. Kim, P. H., Ferrin, D. L., Cooper, C. D., & Dirks, K. T. (2004). Removing the shadow of suspicion: The effects of apology vs. denial for repairing ability- vs. integrity-based trust violations. *Journal of Applied Psychology, 89*, 104–118.

6. Kim, P. H., Dirks, K. T., Cooper, C. D., & Ferrin, D. L. (2006). When more blame is better than less: The implications of internal vs. external attributions for the repair of trust after a competence- vs. integrity-based trust violation. *Organizational Behavior and Human Decision Processes, 99*, 49–65.

7. McCullough (2008).

8. Kramer, R. M. (2003, October). The harder they fall. *Harvard Business Review, 81*, 58–66.

9. Miller, D. T. (2001). Disrespect and the experience of injustice. *Annual Review of Psychology, 52*, 527–553; Heider, F. (1958). *The psychology of interpersonal relations*. New York: Wiley.

10. Man who posed as Marine hero sentenced to tend military graves. (2007, July 31). *Seattle Post-Intelligencer*.

11. Lelyveld, A. (1971). Punishment: For and against. In A. S. Neill (Ed.), *Punishment: For and against*. New York: Hart.

12. Tripp, T. M., Bies, R. J., & Aquino, K. (2002). Poetic justice or petty jealousy? The aesthetics of revenge. *Organizational Behavior and Human Decision Processes, 89*, 966–984.

13. Bergler, E. (1946). Poetic justice and its unconscious background. *Medical Record, 1*, 548–550.

14. Danow, D. K. (1995). Official and unofficial culture: Verbal art and the art of revenge. *Semiotica, 106,* 245–255.

15. Mayer, R. C., Davis, J. H., & Schoorman, D. F. (1995). An integrative model of organizational trust. *Academy of Management Review, 20,* 709–734. See also Skarlicki, Barclay, & Pugh (2008).

16. For a textbook review, see Lewicki, R. J., Barry, B., & Saunders, D. M. (2006). *Negotiation* (5th ed.). Homewood, IL: Irwin. For a recent empirical demonstration, see Stouten, J., De Cremer, D., & van Dijk, E. (2006). Violating equality in social dilemmas: Emotional and retributive reactions as a function of trust, attribution, and honesty. *Personality and Social Psychology Bulletin, 32,* 894–906. Also see Pease, P. W., Schreiber, A. M., & Taylor, A. W. (2003). Caught telling the truth: Effects of honesty and communication media in distributive negotiations. *Group Decision and Negotiation, 12,* 537–566.

17. Gabarro, J. J., & Kotter, J. P. (1980). Managing your boss: A compatible relationship with your superior is essential to being effective in your job. *Harvard Business Review, 58,* 92–100.

18. Tripp, T. M., & Bies, R. J. (1997). What's good about revenge? The avenger's perspective. In R. J. Lewicki, R. J. Bies, & B. H. Sheppard (Eds.), *Research on negotiation in organizations* (Vol. 6, pp. 145–160). Greenwich, CT: JAI Press.

19. Alinsky, S. (1971). *Rules for radicals: A pragmatic primer for realistic radicals.* New York: Random House.

20. Tjosvold, D. (2008). The conflict-positive organization: It depends on us. *Journal of Organizational Behavior, 29,* 19–28.

21. Milgram, S. (1974). *Obedience to authority: An experimental view.* New York: HarperCollins.

22. Barclay, L. J., & Skarlicki, D. P. (in press). Healing the wounds of organizational injustice: Examining the benefits of expressive writing. *Journal of Applied Psychology.*

23. Takaku, S. (2001). The effects of apology and perspective taking on interpersonal forgiveness: A dissonance-attribution model of interpersonal forgiveness. *Journal of Social Psychology, 141,* 494–508.
24. Tripp & Bies (1997).
25. McCullough (2008).

Chapter Eight

1. Aquino, K., Tripp, T. M., & Bies, R. J. (2001). How employees respond to personal offense: The effects of blame attribution, victim status, and offender status on revenge and reconciliation in the workplace. *Journal of Applied Psychology, 86,* 52–59.
2. Worthington, E., & Scherer, M. (2004). Forgiveness is an emotion-focused coping strategy that can reduce health risks and promote health resilience: Theory, review, and hypotheses. *Psychology and Health, 19,* 385–405. See also Witvliet, C. V. O., Worthington, E. L., Root, L. M., Sato, A. M., Ludwig, T. E., & Exline, J. J. (2008). Retributive justice, restorative justice, and forgiveness: An experimental psychophysiology analysis. *Journal of Experimental Social Psychology, 44,* 10–25; and Worthington, E. L., Witvliet, C. V. O., Pietrini, P., & Miller, A. J. (2007). Forgiveness, health, and well-being: A review of evidence for emotional versus decisional forgiveness, dispositional forgivingness, and reduced unforgiveness. *Journal of Behavioral Medicine, 30,* 291–302.
3. Cloke, K. (1993). Revenge, forgiveness and the magic of mediation. *Mediation Quarterly, 11,* 67–78; Montville, J. V. (1993). The healing function of conflict resolution. In D. J. D. Sandole & H. van der Merwe (Eds.), *Conflict resolution: Theory and practice* (pp. 112–128). New York: Manchester University Press.
4. Axelrod, R. (1984). *The evolution of cooperation.* New York: Basic Books; McCullough, M. L. (2008). *Beyond*

revenge: The evolution of the forgiveness instinct. San Francisco: Jossey-Bass.

5. Bies, R. J. (2008). Peering into the soul of discontent: Forgivable and unforgivable offenses. Working paper, McDonough School of Business, Georgetown University.

6. McCullough (2008).

7. Kraman, S. S., & Hamm, G. (1999). Risk management: Extreme honesty may be the best policy. *Annals of Internal Medicine, 131*, 963–967.

8. Barsella, R. M. (2007, July 2). Sincere apologies are priceless. Nurse.com. Available online: www.sorryworks.net /article50.phtml. Access date: August 1, 2008.

9. Doctor's apology: Evidence or not? (2006, February 2). Provo, Utah, *Daily Herald*.

10. Boraine, A. (2001). *A country unmasked: Inside South Africa's Truth and Reconciliation Commission*. New York: Oxford University Press.

11. Bright, D. S., Fry, R. E., & Cooperrider, D. L. (2007). Forgiveness from the perspectives of three response modes: Begrudgement, pragmatism, and transcendence. *Journal of Management, Spirituality & Religion, 3*, 78–103. See also Fox, S., Bennett, R. J., Tripp, T. M., & Aquino, K. (2008). Why employees forgive their offenders: An empirical test of a typology of forgiveness motives. Working paper. Louisiana Tech University.

12. Bies, R. J. (2008). Peering into the soul of discontent: The forgivable and the unforgivable. Working paper.

13. Fox, Bennett, Tripp, & Aquino (2008).

14. McCullough (2008).

15. Gregoire, Y., & Fisher, R. J. (2006). The effects of relationship quality on customer retaliation. *Marketing Letters, 17*, 31–46.

16. Worthington, E. L., Witvliet, C. V. O., Pietrini, P., & Miller, A. J. (2007). *Journal of Behavioral Medicine, 30*, 291–302, p. 291.

17. Woodstock Theological Center. (1998). *Forgiveness and conflict resolution: Reality and utility*. Washington, DC: Woodstock Center.

18. Exline, J. J., Worthington, E. L., Jr., Hill, P., & McCullough, M. E. (2003). Forgiveness and justice: A research agenda for social and personality psychology. *Personality and Social Psychology Review, 7,* 337–348.

19. Corrado, R. R., Cohen, I. M., Glackman, W., & Odgers, C. (2003). Serious and violent young offenders decisions to recidivate: An assessment of five sentencing models. *Crime & Delinquency, 49,* 179–200; Galaway, B., & Judson, J. (1996). Restorative justice: International perspectives. Monsey, NY: Criminal Justice Press.

20. Knowlton, W. A., & Mitchell, T. R. (1980), Effects of causal attributions on a supervisor's evaluation of subordinate performance. *Journal of Applied Psychology, 65,* 459–566.

21. For instance, see Kerr, S. (1995). On the folly of rewarding A, while hoping for B. *Academy of Management Executive, 9,* 7–14.

22. Wintz, J. (2004). Archbishop Sean P. O'Malley: A new voice in Boston. *St. Anthony Messenger.* Available online: www.americancatholic.org/Messenger/Mar2004/Feature1 .asp. Access date: June 23, 2008.

23. Salmon, J. L. (2008). Pope watch. Available online: http://blog.washingtonpost.com/pope-watch/, Access date: June 23, 2008.

About the Authors

Robert J. Bies is a professor of management and founder of the Executive Master's in Leadership Program at the McDonough School of Business at Georgetown University.

Bies's current research focuses on leadership and the delivery of bad news, organizational justice, and revenge and forgiveness in the workplace. He has published extensively on these topics and related issues in academic journals. He currently serves on the editorial boards of *Journal of Applied Psychology*, *Journal of Organizational Behavior*, *Journal of Management*, *International Journal of Conflict Management*, and *Negotiation and Conflict Management Research*.

Bies has received several teaching awards, including the *Best Teacher* award at Northwestern University's Kellogg School of Management. At Georgetown, he has twice received the *Joseph Le Moine Award for Undergraduate and Graduate Teaching Excellence* at the McDonough School of Business, and he received the *Outstanding Professor of the International Executive MBA Program* (IEMBA-2) at the McDonough School of Business. He received his Ph.D. from Stanford University in organizational behavior, and a B.A. in business administration and an M.B.A. from the University of Washington.

Thomas M. Tripp is a professor of management and operations at Washington State University. Professor Tripp has published dozens of research articles in scientific journals on the subject of workplace conflict and organizational justice. Currently, he is chair of the Conflict Management Division of the Academy of Management, the professional association of nearly twenty thousand management professors. He also serves on the editorial boards of *Negotiations and Conflict Management Research*, *International Journal of Conflict Management*, *Journal of Organizational Behavior*, and the *Journal of Management*.

Tripp has taught courses in leadership skills and in negotiation skills. He has twice received the award for *Outstanding Faculty Teaching* from WSU's College of Business. He also won the *Students' Award for Teaching Excellence* from the WSU Vancouver campus students. Finally, he was inducted into WSU's Teaching Academy as one of twelve inaugural members, and served as its vice chair.

He received a Ph.D. in organizational behavior from the Kellogg School of Management at Northwestern University, and a B.S. in psychology from the University of Washington. Born and raised in Seattle, he continues to live in the Pacific Northwest.

Index